THE INVISIBLE WEDDING

It is only with the heart that one can see rightly,
what is essential is invisible to the eye.

—Antoine de Saint-Exupery

The INVISIBLE WEDDING

EXPLORING THE ESSENCE OF SPIRITUAL PARTNERSHIP

David and Faye Fields

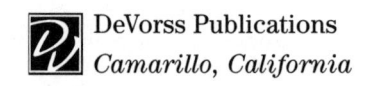

DeVorss Publications
Camarillo, California

We dedicate this work of
The Invisible Wedding to Amma,
for healing the world, one hug at a time.

Library of Congress Cataloging-in-Publication Data
Fields, David, 1952–
The invisible wedding : exploring the essence of spiritual partnership/
David and Faye Fields.
p. cm.
ISBN 0-87516-793-4
1. Interpersonal relations—Religious aspects.
I. Fields, Faye, 1953– II. Title.
BL626.33.F54 2004
204'.41—dc22
2004043914
First Edition, 2004

Printed in the United States of America

DeVorss & Company, Publisher
P.O. Box 1389
Camarillo, California 93011-1389
www.devorss.com

Contents

Acknowledgments

We have been blessed with much heartfelt support over the last many years together. First and foremost, we offer our gratitude to our spiritual teachers for pointing the way: to Amma for Her limitless, undying, love for all creation. And to Nisargadatta Maharaj, Ramesh Balsekar, and Wayne Liquorman, for pointing so eloquently to the One underlying the two.

Thank you DeVorss & Company, especially Gary Peattie, for his love and commitment to this work. And Laura Golden Bellotti for her brilliant editorial gifts.

Thank you to all the dear ones who have been present for us and our healing work in the world: Juanita Crampton and Jan Rhine (true sisters and Godmothers to our children). David Speck and Val Berry-Speck for their love of God and prayers for us during our own very dark night. Brenda Huson for her tenderness over all these years. David Taylor for opening his heart and his door to us some twelve years ago. Steve Smith for great friendship and artistic vision. And Ron Mink for his constant satsang and healing vibes over these last twenty years!

And thank you to Greg Vergets for high conversations about women. Leonard Orr for modeling innocence, gentleness and conscious breathing. Leonard Cohen for songs of mercy and for soulful sharing about lonesome trailers, kids, and Zen while hanging out in Bombay, along with Gabriel and Singh. Howard Wade for thirty years of encouragement and editorial support. To our children, Julian, Lawrence, Angela, and Nathan, for their pure teachings on unconditional love. And to all the known and unknown yogis and tantric sages who have kept the fire of Truth blazing in this world. All credit to the One!

Introduction

Let yourself be silently drawn
by the stronger pull of what
you really love.
—RUMI

In 1978 David and I met for the first time on a meditation retreat. There was a hint of soul recognition in the eyes when we were introduced by friends, but nothing could have prepared us for the changes ahead. Six months later, in the spring of 1979, the river of life brought us together again. Our worlds exploded. We fell deeply in love. It was a profound catalyst and would change almost every aspect of our lives.

Along with the ecstasy of coming together was the heartbreak of saying goodbye to loved ones, as we were both married at the time. Also, though we had only met recently, both of us had been students of the same spiritual teacher for many years. Somehow the intensity of our coming together synchronized with a need to say farewell to this teaching. Its emphasis on meditation as the sole means to enlightenment no longer spoke to the heart of our relationship and the tandem journey on which we now found ourselves. We grieved the loss of spiritual family and the affection we felt for our teacher, but there was no turning back.

At times our new love was disorienting, like being in a boat on the high seas. But a master plan was beginning to reveal itself. This new love was helping to mend a split—albeit an invisible one—at the very core of our hearts.

Our romance gradually gave way to periods of strife, as it does for most people. Powerful feelings of safety would suddenly flip over to equally powerful feelings of doubt and suspicion. Like a cosmic roller-coaster, love and fear seemed to be intertwined. Whereas in our previous relationships conflict between ourselves and our other partners had been suppressed, now somehow we were pulled to investigate it. We were fully committed to making our relationship work. We pondered: What causes the ritual opening and closing of our hearts? From where does the urge to blame arise? What is the source of desire? Where is the true source of love? How can we nurture a wholesome, loving relationship?

Asking ourselves such questions, we began to fathom together the depths of heart, mind, and body. So intense was our quest in the early years that at times we felt like deep-sea divers. We built fires during the winter and stayed up all night sharing, meditating, and making love. Our investigation consumed countless layers of emotional and physical armor as we exposed our deepest wounds to one another, and in the process, touched our most tender essence. But it was not always easy, and it was not free of pain.

Romance is deceptive. Like most new lovers, we came together with an unconscious fantasy that we had finally found the one person who truly understood us. We had met the one mate who would never betray our trust or judge us. Little did we know at the time that our sense of certainty about our love for one another had to be shattered before we could experience the bloom of real love.

Just three years after coming together, David became seriously ill. For the next several years we lived on the brink of physical, emotional and financial collapse. I had not only to care for David, but our son Julian as well, who was just turning two years old. Several months into the ordeal, old wounds reemerged like thunderstorms. Buried feelings of anger, resentment, blame and guilt surfaced with great ferocity. As David spent entire days resting and often depressed, I grieved the loss of a once-joyful, creative partner with whom to co-parent, play, and enjoy life. The apparent needs that had brought us together were no longer able to be met, and our egos rioted. During this time we made the painful discovery of how easily human love—based on ego—can turn to hate! But as our predicament unfolded, we turned increasingly from healing the body to a deep concern for the heart. It was here, in the heart, that the real work lay.

After decades of resistance, and with our defenses finally down, we began to face the unhealed scars of the respective emotional battles from our past. It required the ordeal of David's illness to make us aware that we had brought to our relationship (among other more wholesome aspects) exactly what had not been healed from our pasts. We were delivered to a place that could no longer deny our broken hearts.

Gradually, as the illness refused to let up, David's past—the hurt and neglect of growing up with alcoholic parents—thawed from around his heart. What began with outbursts of frustrated anger and criticism toward me and him, eventually turned into tears of grief and longing for the care he never experienced when he was a child.

Exhausted by the role of caregiver and healer, my own awareness was forced inward for soul food. What began with intense resentment toward David for his apparent inability to meet my emotional needs gradually turned into a deeper investigation of the heart. I had to face the root causes and feel the pain associated with my endless need for love, approval, and appreciation from others.

Through the ordeal of long-term illness, our attention was pointed inward, and we became aware of core needs that truly had nothing to do with the other person. These needs had to do with deepening our own inner centers, forgiving self and others for past abuses, facing the fear that turns into judgment, finding the healer and nurturer within ourselves and, ultimately, feeling the love of God pulsating in our hearts.

We had never been taught that, as a couple, we would somehow have to journey into the Land of Death together (and this would not be the only time, or the only way). But it was actually there, in the heavy darkness, that love bloomed. It bloomed when we took each other off the cross of expectation and turned within to face the root of our pain. Love bloomed when we stopped looking for it externally or in each other. It was our first death together, and it broke open our tender, once guarded, hearts.

Through the intensity of our experience, and years of counseling couples professionally, it has become clear that we all carry within us the invisible pain of a broken heart. This wound manifests most clearly in our neurotic search for love and approval from others. Rather than turning inward when we feel pain or unloved, we are trained to look outside for our fulfillment. In an attempt to avoid the pain of their broken hearts, many seek special relationships with those who foster in us a false sense of well-being. David and I are no exception.

Our relationship and our healing work have taught us that it is not enough for the heart to heal bad childhoods. Nor is it enough to find an "ideal" partner. As a foundation for every other type of healing, we must reawaken our spiritual core.

In every human being, the original heartbreak has to do with the apparent divorce from our deepest spiritual essence, or the Beloved, as we poetically refer to it. As the ego develops in childhood, we lose touch with our essence and no longer feel connected to life as a whole. This involves a subtle shift away from the mystical, intuitive nature of the heart to the materialistic, rational way of the head. All relationship issues, no matter how intricate or unique, eventually reflect this primal wound. Feeling separate, small, inadequate, we unconsciously assume various masks in the process of becoming adults. Some stitch on a cheerful face to hide their sadness. Others wear a frown to hide their essential joy. Some learn to take charge. Others learn to be passive. Some become aloof. Others crave contact. Some become pleasers. Others become rebels. Some become fiercely independent. Others become hopeless romantics. Each is a different mask, an unconscious strategy to guard the tender, nonjudgmental nature of the heart hidden below. Add to this portrait faulty parenting, bad teachers, various traumatic experiences, and a culture in denial of the sacred, and it becomes extremely difficult to consciously reconnect to our once vital essence. Before long we lose touch with the melody of Wholeness within and instead live with the sense that we are no longer truly loved.

This core feeling of being essentially unloved is what sets most of us off on a life-long search for that special someone

who can reawaken the internal feeling of being fully, unconditionally loved again. We go on seeking love, approval, and appreciation from others until—often as the result of a personal
crisis—our attention once again turns inward and we realize
that love is not somewhere out there. No one can truly give us
love. It dwells beyond the mind's conditioning, within our
own hearts. Love is who we are in essence, and it lays the invisible groundwork for an authentic, loving relationship.

Once we begin to realize that the true Beloved lies within,
an enormous burden is lifted from our relationship; our partners are taken off the unbearable cross of needing to make us
happy. Conflict gets resolved at its source—in the mending of
our own inner hearts. Now we are joined like a sacred triangle,
with the Beloved at the apex and each of us at the base. From
here there is no other reason to relate intimately except for the
joy of sharing the full journey of life. We embrace together a
path that will inevitably include an abundance of tears and
laughter, pleasure and pain, life and death. We simply dance
with life together.

The Beloved is our essential Self, our intrinsic Wholeness. It
dwells in the innermost stillness of our hearts, in the absence
of ego or mind. Ego (mind) in the context we use it, is simply
that part of us that lives in the total belief of separation from
God. This is the ultimate abandonment—beyond any childhood event—that gives rise to fear, doubt, suspicion, and all
manner of discontent. The Invisible Wedding is a mending of
the broken heart, a return to innocence and natural wisdom as
the mind and heart come to rest in balance.

In the pages ahead, we describe this journey in the context
of spiritual partnership. Although we shed plenty of light on
the mind, this book is not primarily about a psychological

journey. We do not teach you how to cleverly negotiate the needs that arise in your relationship. We do not teach you strategies for getting all the approval, praise, and acceptance you might want from your partner. *The Invisible Wedding: Exploring the Essence of Spiritual Partnership* is a compass that points us to a place within that is already whole. The real marriage is to the Beloved, not our partner, and the wedding happens not in a physical church, temple, or synagogue, but in the sanctuary of our own hearts. As the heart opens to the realization of its immense fullness, a gradual yet spontaneous kindness and generosity are infused into each act we engage in. And each of us is seen for what we are: An exquisite reflection of the Beloved, warts, bruises and battle scars included.

When the heart feels wholesome, everything becomes holy. Sex becomes a passionate communion. We make love with our every gesture, word, hug, meal. We cease our defensive posturing and remain effortlessly open to whatever the moment brings.

As lovers, we come to understand that our capacity for love is always equal to our ability to open to pleasure and pain. This work teaches us how to be present for whatever needs to arise. Only by accepting life fully and embracing all that we are (full of light and dark) can the flower of love sprout, grow, bloom, seed and die again and again in the course of a lifetime. There is nothing to reject on this journey to the Invisible Wedding.

Through our years together—now twenty five—we continue to be amazed at the vastness of Life and the mystery and wonder of it all. We share *The Invisible Wedding* as a way of swapping notes with you on your journey of the heart. It's a hearty meal. Take it slow; eat only what you can digest. We wrote it for the growing family of awakening individuals who want to cultivate a spiritual partnership and who have heard the call of the

True Lover, knowing intuitively that He/She/That dwells ever so perfectly, patiently, in the heart.

This project came together after countless cups of Sattwa Chai, during sacred fire ceremonies and untold hours of discussion. Afterwards, David would retire to the upstairs room to craft our ideas into the book. We've spent many years sitting in counseling sessions with couples, which became much of our source material, along with the intense fathoming
of our own relationship. We offer this book with a prayer to the Beloved that all may have the opportunity to experience the simple mercy of love. May All Beings Be Happy! May All Beings Be Peaceful!

—FAYE FIELDS

THE INVISIBLE WEDDING

PART ONE

The Invitation

CHAPTER ONE

The Fertile Darkness

For even as love crowns you so shall he
crucify you. Even as he is for your growth
so is he for your pruning.
—KAHLIL GIBRAN

Spiritual partnerships are a holy fire. The first intoxicating sense we get is of a great vibrant spaciousness, like sunrise on a mountaintop. The air sparkles fresh, alive, and clean. We step out of a black and white world into bright technicolor. We feel lively, attentive, and full of vigor. We radiate optimism and passion. Romance is a great high, a glimpse into an unfettered quality of heart. But often such feelings begin to fade.

Typically, over time, a cloud of unknowing descends, and we find ourselves entering what might be called *the fertile darkness*, where questions, hard to articulate, float up from deep inside, forcing us to address deeper issues. What is the true purpose of this relationship? Who lives beyond these social masks? To what extent do our needs define or impede our relating? What is the source of the tension and attraction between us? Why are we so happy, and yet afraid? What is this spontaneous, irresistible, irrational, compelling longing that we feel? Love, that strange, winged bird of paradox, is sometimes as painful as it is joyful.

Once such inquiry begins, we cross an invisible boundary, where the fire that will weld us into spiritual partnership is ignited. A force more powerful and pervasive than our rational mind begins pounding at the door of our heart, shattering concepts and stirring up dragons, while the shadows of love dance around us.

THE EXQUISITE MIRROR

Relationships are an exquisite mirror. If we look closely we can witness the ritual opening and closing of our hearts and the myriad ways our minds seek to avoid or embrace the fire of love. We rub up against each other's edges, only to confront the walls of our own imaginings and conceptions. We point self-righteously to the flaws in our partner's character only to discover in honest moments our own vulnerability. As we move deeper into intimacy, the mirror grows sharper. When the spiritual eye begins to open we sense a healing agenda emerging from the space between habitual modes of thought and feeling. Gradually, if we persist and remain open, a brighter something is born—an understanding, a realization—and we find that through the excruciating ordeal of love and intimacy our inner hearts and minds are healed. We call this healing part of the Invisible Wedding—invisible because the transformation occurs within, a wedding because the separation inside us is mended. But the whole wedding, as we will explore further on, goes beyond the uniting of mind and heart, to include that of the individual with the Beloved.

In a spiritual partnership we explore together the rich fabric of our inner lives. This nurtures not only ourselves but our spouses, children, and community. A heart that learns to authentically love another learns to love all. In more conventional relationships, goals are almost exclusively defined in terms of emotional and material security, whereas in a spiritual partnership the primary target is a deepening realization of wholeness. The sometimes wild, unpredictable investigation of truth becomes more compelling than the ego's need for constant reassurance.

INVESTIGATING OUR FEELINGS, THOUGHTS AND BEHAVIORS

In a spiritual partnership we are challenged to investigate—rather than suppress—uncomfortable thoughts, feelings, and behaviors that inevitably arise in the context of relating. Even for couples already on a spiritual journey there is often the sense that life *should* be different than what it is. We *shouldn't* be jealous that our partner is hanging out with friends after work. We *should* be making love more often. We *shouldn't* get so angry. We *shouldn't* experience attractions outside of our primary relationship. The list goes on. Our mental judgments and imaginings are constantly battling with the reality of what is. Such judgments originate from the ego's fundamental insecurity and its chronic need for assurance and control. All such issues once welcomed in as part of our investigation into ourselves, become powerful catalysts for personal insight and deepening intimacy.

Healing begins with an *acceptance of what is*, including our own judgments and oscillating states of mind. To heal anger we must acknowledge it. To make peace with fear we must welcome its presence. To calm jealousy we must view it without self-judgment and condemnation. Once we set a place at the table for our demons, perhaps they will no longer torment us. Once we stop trying to control or manipulate the phenomena that fill our psychic and physical space, perhaps we can begin to heal and experience a level of intimacy beyond words. But such a path will take us beyond our personalities, with all their likes and dislikes. If we go far enough with our investigation we will meet in a place beyond the conditional nature of the ego.

A basic principle that we will explore throughout these pages is that healing and real intimacy happen from the level of the spirit, not the ego. This is why Western psychology often fails to restore wholeness to the individual. Caught in a mechanistic paradigm, it often does not acknowledge the transpersonal, intuitive heart within which mind, body, spirit, and environment are wed. It is this unifying vision in the context of intimate sharing that we will explore in *The Invisible Wedding*.

Recognizing the Beloved

Ron and Terry were students in college when they were caught in Cupid's sights. Their every spare moment was consumed in that fragile yet holy rapture in which new lovers find themselves—making love, sharing dreams, telling personal stories long into the night. No hurdle was too high, no hang-up too severe to be overcome. It was not long before they were spending evenings anxiously planning their wedding. Once they completed graduate studies in music Ron would get a job teaching at a university in Colorado. Terry would work in an orchestra for a few years before committing to a family. Their plans carried them blissfully into the next decade.

Six months into their relationship, as they were driving home on the last rainy night of their honeymoon, they crashed their car. Ron was paralyzed from the waist down, and Terry was abruptly cast into the role of round-the-clock caregiver. Their idealized relationship, and all their cherished plans and dreams, had suddenly exploded like a star.

Following the accident, a profound, heart-rending inquiry into their love began. The bright romantic face of the Beloved that first tickled them into relating had been exciting, even liberating, but clearly not substantial enough to deal with the demands of their present circumstances. They would have to mine deep within the heart for the spiritual understanding that would help them transcend their current terrifying predicament.

What had caused this tragic event, they pondered. How do we survive? How do we now relate to each other? How do we make love when one of us cannot even move a toe? What does it mean to love another? Who or what is in charge here? In fact, who or what in essence are we?

Such questioning ripped at the old conditioning like a wolf eating caribou. Love, they learned, caters neither to expectations nor unconscious needs for security. Although their first attraction had been physical, it was not the body that lit up their hearts. While they had charmed each other with their musical gifts, it was not the violin that made them dance. Only when their awareness opened to *the Beloved*—to the spiritual heart and source within—did they finally understand the meaning of love.

One evening when Terry had gone out to a movie, Ron's wheelchair tipped, throwing him to the floor. When Terry finally returned shortly before midnight, she discovered Ron lying bruised and helpless in the bathroom. Instead of showing her usual concern and compassion, she exploded at him, releasing a dam of emotion fueled by the enormous burden she had silently carried these many months since the accident. With contorted face and pointing finger she scolded him for his negligence, his carelessness. She accused him of not considering all the care and effort she had given to him.

Ron at once felt the sting of her attack, but as he prepared his rebuttal, something suddenly turned inside him. His guard dropped and what was anger shifted to a deeper sense of understanding. Like a fog lifting, he saw that Terry's upset was not truly at him but toward herself. The anger, he realized, came from a sense of deep helplessness, from an utter loss of control. Life had become an animal neither one could tame. In the rawness of that moment Ron saw it all quite clearly. Abruptly his mind ceased its frenzied search. How simple it was. Healing, in the deepest sense, had nothing to do with outer circumstances. Instead, it was an inner recognition that awakened an effortless, unconditional *acceptance of life as it is*, here and now. In that moment Ron was home, where he had, in fact, always resided. He realized that there was nowhere to go and nothing to do. The Spirit, the untainted essence that resides within, had always been whole, content, and free. He saw that healing was not on the level of any physical condition but in the recognition of his own spiritual essence. From his new vantage point he and Terry were already whole. Although his legs were still limp, Ron had never felt more free and peaceful and content in his life. His only response was to smile and gently reach out a hand.

Ron's presence opened like a warm sea around Terry. Instead of punishment, she was greeted with the deepest possible acceptance. Instead of harsh defenses, she was embraced by unconditional love. Suddenly an uncontainable sorrow surfaced from inside. Her once furrowed brows softened as she began to weep. Terry finally saw that no matter how hard she tried, she could not heal this man, her husband, through her own will power. She could not restore his sense of wholeness with her prayers and efforts because, in fact, he was not broken. A tension released inside Terry's body, and with several deep sighs, she simply surrendered. She was no longer her husband's keeper. She was his spiritual companion.

Gently Terry reached down, saw Ron gazing upward, and together they wrestled his body back into the chair. For the next several hours they shared and listened to one another as never before. The clouds were gone, and from their hearts they made true confession. It was all about their previously erroneous perceptions. They had mistakenly defined themselves in terms of a broken body, an empty bank account, a world unsympathetic to the handicapped, a separate, frightened ego. And from that first mistake countless other notions were born, all of which amounted to a refusal to accept the simple reality of *what is*. Instead, frustrated, scared, believing that things ought to be different, and hoping that one day they would, they were trying to hold onto shallow identities carved out of the past that were now at war with the present. Their previous expectations and frustrated selves vanished with the recognition of this new found wholeness. Their inner sense of wholeness, which revealed itself as they turned within to their essence, is what we refer to poetically as *the Beloved*.

When we connect with the Beloved our minds become quiet and accepting, and we realize that the present moment contains everything we need. No circumstance, no person can either add to or subtract from what we are in essence. This insight has profound, far-reaching consequences in the way we relate to life. We no longer push the river. We no longer cling to loved ones as life-lines. We no longer enter into relationships with hidden agendas based on getting. Instead, we become open, relaxed and joyful, and delighted to share the journey. The Beloved is the invisible key to loving relationships.

From that moment on Ron and Terry no longer felt the compulsive need to change either their circumstances or each other. Their situation was not always ideal, but they accepted it. They realized that neither of them was essentially broken. No one needed fixing. For the first time they both understood what it meant to be peaceful and content in the moment. The seeking of something better ceased. There were times when they would be sad or when they would be happy, but no longer was there the painful judgment that things ought to be different. There was a deep, unshakable acceptance.

In the ensuing months Ron interpreted his paralysis not as a hindrance or handicap to living but as a spiritual gift. It had shocked him out of adhering to an ego that constantly looked to the past or future, rather than living in the present. Terry was no longer burdened by a heavy sense of her husband's paralysis but saw herself engaged in a powerful *yoga of the heart*. Her creative edge was to see the perfect face of the Beloved in whatever form was present. Together, they ceased paying attention to the unending frenzy of the mind.

On that crucial evening when Ron fell from his wheelchair, he and Terry awakened to the spiritual heart of relating. They had met their true *Lover* and together they celebrated. A spiritual partnership was forged that reflected a new alliance between their hearts and minds.

Ron and Terry's story reflects the need many of us feel to re-focus our lives internally. Suffering is predicated on the belief that fulfillment lies in a relationship with something outside of us, with an *other*—whether this *other* is the right partner, a solid bank account, a new car, a healthy body, or the perfect job. Contrary to the continuous media messages injected daily into our collective brain, no thing, no person, no object has any ability to satisfy that longing for love. Love is found purely in the heart. It is our essence—as close to us as our own breath.

Romantic love is enticing precisely because through it we sometimes glimpse the intense sweetness of our union with the true Beloved; but it is only a glimpse. The good news is that the wholeness, the unconditional love we are secretly dying for, is *within us*. It is the stillness and silence of the prophets. It is the Beloved adored in the Song of Solomon and the mystic poets like Hafiz and Mirabai. It is the mystic Friend, of Rumi. It does not grow old and it never gets sick or complains. When we are in the throes of romantic love, our partner is, in part, a reflection of this One who constantly dwells within, and yet she or he can neither add to nor subtract from our connection to the Beloved. This insight dispels a tremendous burden from any relationship. A lightness dawns and we begin to share and celebrate in a love that is free, abundant, and unconditional.

Returning Home

The Invisible Wedding is about a return to our original home. It describes the spiritual journey toward a union of heart and mind that two people can take together. As the late mythologist

Joseph Campbell explained once in an interview for PBS with Bill Moyers, "Marriage is the symbolic recognition of our identity—two aspects of the same being." It was this recognition some twenty-five years ago that inspired us to begin a profound and intense exploration of our relationship as a spiritual journey. This book is one of the fruits of that journey.

Perhaps your lives have not been shattered as violently as Ron and Terry's. The process by which your ego gives way to wholeness will likely be slower and gentler. Still, once you begin to focus your attention inward, to the spiritual essence that links us all, you will find yourselves cutting through the same illusions that confronted Ron and Terry. One way or another, we are called on to examine our conditioning with regard to sex, God, happiness, beauty, money, mortality, and the unquenchable needs of mind and body. We will hear the irresistible song of the Beloved, and begin to dance in the fire.

Very few couples take as direct a path to the spiritual heart as Ron and Terry. Most of us travel more gradually, as we discover how to break through the various tensions and memories that cloud our capacity to love and feel loved. But the darkness we enter as we begin this spiritual course is a fertile one. It bears passion fruit for those who make the journey.

In the next chapter we will explore the need for undressing the heart. For intimacy to deepen, we must have the capacity to open fully to whatever resides within us, be it pleasant or painful. It is not always a flowery process, but it is a flowering. The conflict between us can be utilized to open the heart. The passion between us can be the torch to ignite the sacred in every part of our shared life.

CHAPTER TWO

The Naked Heart

For the raindrop, joy is in entering the river—
Unbearable pain becomes its own cure.
—GHALIB

Genuine intimacy is akin to a process of becoming naked. We drop our socially adapted masks and slowly open to the revelation of our hearts. But the path of intimacy can be challenging. As our hearts open wider, the wounds, negative beliefs and shame from our past rise to the surface—and we are called upon to investigate them. Intimacy is a window into ourselves.

During the first year of our marriage, some twenty-five years ago, my (David's) heart suddenly encountered a profound state of vulnerability. We were exploring techniques of extended lovemaking. By taking the emphasis off the typical goal of climaxing, we learned to relax deeper into the rapture and bliss of the moment. We discovered that sex, when engaged in from a quieter, meditative perspective, could be a delightful doorway into the sacred, into deep spiritual communion.

At the end of this one occasion, lying in each other's warm, sweaty arms, I was suddenly hit with a rush of intense fear. Terror is perhaps a better word. I found myself literally shaking like a leaf inside and struggled to stay in control. I wanted to hide, but fortunately, there was nowhere to go. The more I tried to resist the feelings the more intense they became. A force far more powerful than my conscious mind had taken over. Resistance was futile. My breathing became rapid, and I began to shake as if attempting to get free from some unknown internal restriction. What was this fear? Why was I afraid to be seen?

The fear, in part, was the initial vulnerability of a closed heart starting to open to the unknown; it was the terror of having gone deep together, of sharing much, of being stripped both physically and emotionally before the unclouded eyes of my beloved. My defenses rioted. What if she judges me? What if I'm rejected? What if I can't let go? This fear was the death cry of my ego that wanted to be in control as our boundaries dissolved and the sense of I merged into a We. Suddenly, like countless lovers and mystics before us, the duality of self and other was collapsing. As I finally relaxed—and felt into the fear—the shaking subsided and we found ourselves entering a profound level of intimacy. We had caught a glimmer of the naked heart. But it was only a beginning. The experience, which would repeat itself countless times in different ways over the years, had much to teach us.

How is it that love brings up fear? As long as we base our sense of being loved on an other, we will inevitably find ourselves caught in the painful grips of contraction and expansion. Our loving—and the need to be loved—will be tinged, however subtly, with the fear of loss. The way of intimacy is not to renounce or deny need, but to accept it as part of the opening and listen for where it leads. It is a facet of what we encounter in the undressing of the heart.

Love and vulnerability are often intertwined. Old hurts, traumas and memories get reenergized the deeper we open to one another. There is risk. A spiritual partnership can be frightening—and transformative—because real intimacy dissolves barriers, at times reflecting whatever unmet needs stand in the way of wholeness. As we open to each other we are challenged each step of the way to first embrace, then look beyond our neediness to the deeper truth of the heart. When we listen to our hearts, this truth chants a silent, unending, verse: I am the Beloved. The Beloved is mine. The presence of love we feel with our partner is a reflection of that which resides within us.

For such authentic love to flower, we need to investigate our fear. At the deepest level it arises from the primal thought of a separate me. It forms with the development of the ego and a movement away from the heart. Painful experiences early on further reinforce this duality.

For example, a child quietly reading a book is suddenly the target of verbal or physical abuse by her enraged mother. Terrified, she runs into her bedroom, separating physically from the experience. However, she is still frightened inside. When the situation calms down the child sneaks into the kitchen looking for a snack, not because she needs food, but because she is still frightened and feels the need to also separate emotionally from the experience. Before long her awareness is no longer connected to the original feeling. On the surface she feels more at ease. But deep inside, her basic sense of separateness—along with the accompanying fear—has been reinforced. The primary need for love has been obscured by a secondary need for food. Years later she ponders the cause of her eating disorder and why she craves—yet runs from—intimacy. Deep within resides the unresolved pain associated with her mother and the root feeling of being unloved.

Does everyone carry such a primal wound? What about those of us who came from more nurturing, caring environments?

Even in such circumstances, when we investigate deeply into the nature of the mind, we find a basic knot of unhappiness, a feeling that we are somehow not whole or fully loved. This primal sense of being unloved arises with the development of the ego, and the perception that we are separate from life as a whole. There is a poignant verse in the Upanishads from India that points to this predicament. It states simply that fear arising from duality is the cause of suffering. This duality—self versus other—kicks in around age two as we begin the awkward process of differentiating from our environment. Psychology labels this stage "the terrible twos," because our egos are developing and we begin to show preferences, make judgments, and strive for independence. The price for developing our individuality and defining our boundaries is that we feel increasingly separate from the whole of life, and a subtle suffering arises. Our separateness and suffering grow together and are reinforced in childhood by painful, frightening, or overwhelming events.

It is natural to want to remove ourselves—separate—from anything (a thought, feeling, person, or event) perceived as threatening. In the above example, the child naturally tried to separate from the pain associated with the mother. But in doing so, her ego's basic sense of separateness was reinforced, generating yet more fear and consequently more suffering.

It is in the context of such experiences that core beliefs come into play. Our thoughts crystallize around powerful emotional experiences, reinforcing and defining ourselves as separate entities. Depending on our unique set of experiences, thoughts like, *I can never get enough, Life is not safe, The people I love abandon me, I have to fight to survive, Feeling this pain will kill me, I'm special and nobody appreciates me, I cannot trust anyone, If I fully accept myself, he (she) will leave, I must stay in control to be safe,* get etched into the nervous system and act as lenses through which we interpret, create, and reinforce our sense of duality. All such limiting concepts (and corresponding emotional imprints) hinge on the core sense of being separate. Defensive emotional patterns like blame, denial, and chronic anger form around our core beliefs in an attempt to further distance ourselves and avoid the undischarged pain of the original situation. As a result, we learn to look outside ourselves to others (always without fulfillment) for love and acceptance, even though we fear the exposure of deep intimacy.

As a spiritual partnership unfolds, deeper layers of the ego and its various core beliefs and reactive emotional patterns arise. In learning to trust our experience, to open into it no matter how painful (a theme that we will explore repeatedly in the following pages), our underlying sense of separateness and accompanying fear gradually gets dissolved. This is the gift of intimate caring. As defenses drop and the heart gradually opens again, we begin to love with fewer conditions; we see beyond the persona into the pristine essence of our deeper spiritual character. At this core (soul) level everyone shines immaculate. But to live this understanding requires that we take the full journey. At times we are led into the dark, yet we must reach the point in our growth where we fully accept the invitation to heal.

On the journey of spiritual partnership, most of us will spiral through three distinct phases from romance, through disillusionment, to acceptance.

ROMANCE

Falling in love is a gift of Nature which can, for some, open the door of the heart. It is an unconscious way of reconnecting to our deeper soul essence. The Swiss psychiatrist Carl

Jung described falling in love as a projection of our idealized inner male/female. We speak of it in terms of catching a glimpse of the positive face of the Beloved. Such an experience can be a tremendous catalyst for growth and for some a touchstone into the realm of deep feeling. As we contemplate the nature of falling in love, we find that in its most positive light it is accompanied by a profound sense of being loved, and this is one of its most cherished gifts. The spiritual challenge (opportunity) in romance is to reabsorb or own the projection; that is, to recognize that the beauty we perceive in our partner is a reflection of our own essence. It resides within us, not outside.

Feelings of inadequacy, loneliness, and fear disappear at this stage as we fuse with our partner. However, our ego is only partially submerged. In romance our center or wholeness is projected outside us. Eventually our partners will act in ways that no longer satisfy our ego needs, and again we will find ourselves thrown into doubt and insecurity. At that point, instead of our partners being a cause for our euphoria, we perceive them to be the cause of our suffering. Our projection shifts from that of the Beloved, to the Shadow. We call this second phase of a relationship, disillusionment, and it carries with it a heavy feeling of disappointment. It is at this point that many lovers feel a strong urge to run.

DISILLUSIONMENT

Disillusionment is marked by periodic feelings of separateness, emotional contraction, and disappointment. It is as if the brightness of the Beloved we experienced in the romantic phase now begins to unravel the ego and its attendant shadow. Our partners behave in ways that no longer seem to meet our needs, and suddenly we are plunged into old familiar patterns of negativity. Only now—in contrast to the high of being in love—that negativity is magnified. The sense of being deeply loved so common in romance now shifts at times to fear, frustration and irritability.

The seeds of disillusionment are sown in romance. Anytime our source of love is perceived as external, we will feel insecure, and our ego will riot. Behaviors of control and manipulation—demanding, complaining, seeking approval, threatening, begging—arise in an attempt to bind and control our object of love. The once high emotional need for adoration and unconditional acceptance suddenly switches into a need for punishment and blame. Disillusionment also arises with the dawning realization—however much denied—that our relationship cannot truly give us what we want most: The permanent feeling of being unconditionally loved.

When we experience disillusionment, the healing effect of intimacy has dissolved our defenses and forced to the surface whatever unfinished psychological business is stored in our emotional bodies, or, as Eckhart Tolle refers to it in *The Power of Now*, as the pain body.

In disillusionment our concept of a spiritual partnership must expand to include this disappointment and the coexistence of opposites, the positive and negative, light and dark aspects of the personality. Here we start revealing to our partner and ourselves all those nasty faces we try so hard to keep hidden, such as jealousy, envy, fear, pride, and impatience. Although from the ego's perspective such exposure is a highly painful process, from the spiritual perspective it is all part of the raw and rugged nature of coming home to the heart. We have to face the ego—and all its hidden nooks and crannies of unmet needs—to dismantle it and allow the heart to open. We have to admit our emotional needs in order to finally hear our deepest, heartfelt ones. Our partners become an excellent mirror for the process.

Let's say that in a vulnerable moment—perhaps we've just heard some bad news—we reach out to our partner for support, but he is emotionally unavailable. The child in us rebels, and we attempt to make our partner feel guilty in order to get our needs met. The water between us muddies and a fight ensues. When our partner finally complies with our demand, the conflict subsides, but the root of the matter has not been addressed, and an even greater tension will arise in the future over an apparently different issue. What we learn in the disillusionment phase of a relationship is to look within ourselves in the initial moment of conflict. The source of tension resides within. We may insist that our partners are the source of our discomfort, the undoing of our romance. But a deeper investigation will reveal that we are mirrors for one another. We heal as our hearts are able to remain present and unguarded in the face of all manner of discomfort and pain that might arise between us. When what we see in the other can be embraced as unconscious aspects of ourselves, disillusionment dissolves into the third stage of relating called *Acceptance*. It is in acceptance that we find peace.

ACCEPTANCE

As we come to accept the various states of mind, both positive and negative, that arise in the context of our relationship, a sense of peace gradually arises, and we enter the third phase of relating that we call Acceptance. In this stage we reabsorb—own—our projections. We come to the realization that nobody can actually give us anything, neither heartache nor love, that does not already potentially abide within ourselves. In other words, the unconditional love we once sought in the external (our lover) is now understood to reside inside our own hearts. This removes an enormous burden from the relationship as our partners are no longer held responsible for our well-being. At the deepest level of acceptance our love is no longer based on an other. This creates a sense of spaciousness, freedom, and spontaneity.

The sense of being held in the kind of love that was initially glimpsed in romance now returns, only now we experience it as arising from within our own nature. We discover that the heart of relating is not really about our external lover, but the Self or Beloved within. Rumi goes right to the heart of the matter when he proclaims: The Beloved is all that lives. The lover a dead thing. This is an extraordinary statement! And potent enough to make most conventional relationships quake. Rumi is pointing to the Invisible Wedding. He's telling us that this thing called love is not really about the person sitting over there in the chair. Rather it is the unique presence residing between us and in our hearts. When our partners are no longer seen as objects of love—and therefore not the source of love—all the various strategies of control and manipulation relax. We begin to accept them just the way they are and no longer need anybody to be a certain way in order to feed and reinforce our sense of security. We become spiritual companions on the journey of self-unfoldment. We become lovers of God together. We realize that our relationship is a vehicle for the sacred process of dismantling the armor around the heart and finding the Beloved within. At this point we have discovered the real yoga of relationship.

Finally, we come to accept the inevitability of change and the cyclic nature of life, and love. Life, death, and rebirth are cycles present at every level and each stage of being. We realize that for love to bloom, it must also die. A committed, long-term relationship will undergo many phases of destruction, disillusionment, and rebirth into new life and expression. As spiritual companions, we learn to accept the nature of things with patience and curiosity.

It can be helpful to see the three stages of relating as spiral rather than linear. Various degrees of romance, disillusionment, and acceptance arise and fall away over and over again as the intimacy between us deepens, as the heart continues to open further. So long as the concept of a separate, isolated me exists, there necessarily will be the other with whom we seek to romance, negotiate and, at times, spar.

We can also view spiritual partnerships as a dance with three separate movements. Clearly, the critical stage for most of us is disillusionment. Nobody enjoys confronting the raw and rugged nature of the ego. But there is a highly creative side to disillusionment and the conflict that often accompanies it. We can utilize the energy present in conflict to cut through the mind's resistance and undress the heart. In this sense, conflict can be a positive force.

Conflict can be perceived as a kind of healing crisis, in which the negativity that was hidden in our unconscious is brought to light so we can examine and release it Conflict highlights our unconscious patterns and can be a means of insight. Let us explore in greater detail the concept of the healing crisis and the important role it plays in the context of a spiritual partnership.

call them in their insightful book *Undefended Love*. Our cracked identities are woven from all the various compensatory traits we take on in response to overwhelming childhood experiences.

To compensate for feelings of inadequacy, we might compulsively seek approval and consensus from our partners. To compensate for feelings of powerlessness, we might become a dominating personality. To compensate for a lack of self-worth, we might take on the personality of a do-gooder, somebody who rigidly needs to be on the helping end of the relationship. Behind each compensatory mask lie painful feelings associated with previous unresolved events. Beyond the pain lies our essence. If, in order to avoid our pain, we only relate to each other on the surface of our personality, our relationship eventually becomes unfulfilling, because we never share in the discovery of our essence, our wholeness.

During a healing crisis, defenses start to dissolve, and this pain stored in the unconscious surfaces. From the ego's perspective, we are our cracked identities; thus any new experience or information that threatens our image threatens our survival. Resistance can be very powerful. In the thick of a healing crisis, core beliefs arise with a vengeance.

Here is a list of some common core beliefs.

- I can't trust her.
- The people I love reject me.
- If I just wait long enough the pain will go away.
- Nobody loves me.
- He can't understand how I feel.
- I don't deserve to be loved.

- All women want is to control me.
- I have to stay in control.
- Every time I'm vulnerable I get hurt.
- Love means loss.
- If I fully accept myself, he/she will leave.
- I have to leave or I'll suffocate.

Such feelings of fear, inadequacy, of being out of control arise as part of the healing energy generated by our intimacy. Our relationship is allowing us to access the core energies of our cracked identities. We can use this energy to face our discomfort and deepen our intimacy. The key lies in leaning into our pain, not away from it into thought and analysis.

For spiritual seekers, eyes-closed meditation is not generally the appropriate direction during a crisis. We want to stay in touch with each other and with what we're feeling. We must resist the desire to escape.

THE POWER OF THE PRESENT MOMENT

Reactive patterns, which are composed of both emotional content and mental core beliefs, are rooted in the energy of unreleased past experiences. To the extent that we identify with them, we are virtually living in the past. Therefore, the key to cutting through such patterns is to bring a relaxed awareness into the moment. The illusive past cannot survive the clarity and presence of the moment. In relaxed awareness, we simply accept whatever is arising, whether it is fear, grief, anger, resentment, or the desire to withdraw.

As we mentioned earlier, we became more intimate with each other when we surrendered to or relaxed into the uncomfortable feelings that surfaced after we made love. Staying present with each other, remaining unguarded, we learned that the fears released were not founded in the here and now but rather arose from past experiences of abandonment, loss of love, and rejection rooted in the ego. The intensity of our connection allowed our fears to surface from the unconscious and to finally be released by staying in the present moment. Although our impulse was to shut down emotionally, we didn't give into it. Rather than avoid our feelings, we brought our attention to them. The end result was deeper intimacy.

From countless similar experiences we learned not to hold back from one another, to keep our hearts open, to let go, and to follow whatever feelings arise in the present moment. Feelings, no matter how negative or intense, lead us back to a sense of love if we can stay fully present—remaining unguarded and non-defensive. The inner feeling of being deeply held in love is more basic than that of fear and will win out when we can welcome into awareness whatever wants to arise. We actually are delivered into a space in the heart beyond our relationship. We touch our own essence.

It can be helpful to reflect on certain key points during times of healing crisis.

- Conflict highlights past wounds and is thus a doorway into deeper healing.
- We are never upset for the reason we think we are.
- What we least like in our partner is that which we most need to accept about ourselves.

- When we recognize a core belief, we should ask ourselves: Is this really true?

- Watch out for blame. When you catch yourself blaming, ask the question: What am I avoiding in myself right now?

- Feeling the "need for space" is often an unconscious code for "needing to communicate."

- When you find yourself making an assumption about your partner, ask yourself: Can I absolutely know this to be true?

- Defensiveness is a signpost put up by our ego to indicate that we are entering fertile unknown territory. We cannot enter the new and remain guarded. We must become naked. We start by accepting even our defensiveness.

- When we can remain present in the midst of intense fear and pain, we are delivered to a space in the heart beyond the ego needs of the relationship. When we know intuitively that we don't need our partner in order to be whole, we become truly present for the dance.

By quietly pondering any one of these points our attention will be brought back to our center and the tension between us will begin to dissolve. However, once the conflict escalates beyond a certain point it will probably be too late to quietly contemplate internal causes. This is what we mean by healing crisis. We will have to ride the rapids, so to speak, caught up in the mess of it all, until enough of the emotional charge has been released to engage in self-reflection.

Any kind of discomfort that arises between us can be approached as an opportunity. Each time we are able to bring our attention to a reactive pattern the strength of our attention will grow, and the pattern will diminish. Attention and reactive patterns are mutually exclusive. Attention exists only in the moment. A reactive pattern is rooted in the past and cannot survive the clarity of this moment.

Just as in the natural healing of the body it is vital that we not suppress physical symptoms as they arise, so in the psychology of our relationship we need to challenge the tendency to play it safe by suppressing the arising of reactive patterns. We want to develop the capacity to face whatever thoughts and feelings arise. As our attention steadies, deeper patterns will arise and get dissolved. As attention becomes subtle we can catch a reactive pattern before we go over the edge into healing crisis. At this point the energy trapped in a potential conflict is released and now becomes available for creative expression. As our attention stabilizes in the heart, our relationship begins to dance with a depth and freedom that defies our cultural conditioning. We relate free of the binding nature of the past.

The yoga of a spiritual partnership teaches us that the cause of tension between us ultimately lies within. The emotional need we find most disturbing in our partner is that which we have not yet faced within ourselves. It's all right—even healthy —to fight it out sometimes. But it is crucial to reflect on our own reactivity. It is crucial that we face our true needs. A need for space is usually pointing to a deeper need for communication. A need for acceptance points to a more essential need for self-love. The need for approval reflects the deeper need to draw support from within.

We need to remember to be kind to ourselves as we undertake the process of deepening our relationship. Uncovering new levels of intimacy can be terrifying as our defenses dissolve and past traumas surface out of need for loving attention.

It helps to view conflict not as a hindrance at all but as an opportunity to outgrow restrictive emotional patterns.

In the mere wink of an eye, we can find ourselves unmasked. Suddenly we might find ourselves facing squarely into the richness of the present moment. Here there is no you as separate from me in the heart. No fear. No expectation. No demand that things be different. We just become a silent witness to the vastness of the Naked Heart and its immense capacity to consume the full spectrum of human life. Any issue, no matter how painful, can be softened by remaining present for it. Granted, this is not always easy. But each time we are able to accept emotional pain, our awareness becomes stronger and more flexible.

Unmasking

Chandra was a vivacious, attractive woman in her late twenties when she and her partner, Will, came to see us about the stress in their relationship. Initially she was upset over the lack of sexual intimacy. Apparently they never argued or raised their voices with one another, yet a tension hung in the air around them like smoke.

They explained that their sex life had been fantastic the first year of their relationship but then gradually diminished as Will seemed to lose interest. Chandra correspondingly felt hurt. Deep feelings of inadequacy began to surface, along with painful thoughts that she wasn't desired as a woman. Rather than express her doubts, Chandra explained, she held them in, not wanting to risk further conflict.

The tendency to withhold important information is a form of control and is a way to avoid confronting not only our partners, but ourselves. Control is a basic pattern of unconscious relating. In the attempt to avoid conflict, we perpetuate it. To speak one's truth is to release control, as we can never know the outcome. In conventional relationships, when partners might not be emotionally equipped to handle direct communication, there might be a case for withholding our truth at times. But in a spiritual partnership, except in special cases when it would clearly do more harm to share than not, it is better to confront things head on at the appropriate time. We decided to pose a question, which, initially, took Will and Chandra off center. We asked Chandra what she might be seeking to avoid.

We directed Chandra's attention away from Will and back onto herself. At one point we suggested that Will was possibly acting out an unconscious voice within Chandra that did not want to be sexual. Chandra's brows furrowed in total disbelief. "What? You're suggesting that Will is responding to something in me that doesn't want to be intimate? Bullshit! It's his problem!"

Countless times over the years we have watched the phenomenon of couples acting out each other's unconscious agendas and core beliefs. For instance, a male who unconsciously carries the core belief that women are bitches carefully chooses the sweetest, most congenial woman he can find for a mate. Once the romance fades and they become more honest with each other, she transforms into the Goddess Kali, with giant, disapproving sword in hand! She seems to be on his case about every little thing, from leaving his dirty underwear in the bathroom to being a sloppy pig in the kitchen. It seems he can do nothing right. So long as he avoids the full emotional impact of his suppressed anger toward women and remains unconscious of his core beliefs, this man will repeat the same pattern, regardless of his conscious choice of partners. And unless there is a significant shift inside her, his current partner will continue her disapproval. Whereas the conscious mind looks to surface preferences in choosing a partner, the unconscious meticulously reads the underlying pattern, the hidden content, searching for a fit.

Perhaps a woman abandoned by her father as a young girl carries the belief that men cannot be trusted. She seeks out the most seemingly trustworthy partner she can find, only to repeatedly get her heart broken by betrayal. The pattern continues, regardless of conscious intent, until she is able to acknowledge her core beliefs and finally come to terms with the buried feelings of her original loss.

In Chandra and Will's case, what's happening inside Will that is causing him to not want to make love to his wife? Certainly that question will need to be addressed. But from a broader perspective, our hypothesis is that we are dealing with an unconscious healing agenda in which each partner is playing out a clear, though unacknowledged, role for the other. A more productive question at this point might be: What might Will's behavior be reflecting about Chandra? Although this was a painful and unwanted question, once Chandra moved beyond her initial defensive reaction, she softened, and the feeling between the two of them lightened up. She stopped blaming Will for a moment. Will no longer had the look of guilt and confusion on his face. And while Chandra did not yet acknowledge her own role in their sexual problems, she became open to the possibility of learning more.

For now, we suggested that Chandra just play with another question: Why would she not want to make love to Will? After all, in past relationships with men much less compatible, she always enjoyed an active and supposedly fulfilling sex life.

At this point the mood shifted dramatically. Quiet words sputtered slowly, hesitantly, from her mouth.

Chandra began to share her past experience of having been sexually abused, not yet grasping the connection. Facilitating this session was like carefully cutting away the bandages from a deep and tender wound. Her eyes downcast, barely making contact with us, she revealed the sexual abuse she suffered as a child with her stepfather. Feelings long buried in the unconscious were now laid bare in the healing light of the present. Chandra had been afraid to discuss this with anybody, most of all Will, for fear that she would be seen as impure and no longer sexually desirable.

Shame was the primary emotion that surfaced at this beginning point in her journey. It was the cloud of shame that had kept the secret tucked away inside for all these many years. Now it was surfacing, pressured by the growing intimacy of her relationship to Will. She and Will entered a powerful healing crisis as Chandra's secret became too painful to keep hidden any longer. Had the relationship remained superficial, the wound might never have surfaced, or simply not been recognized as such. They might have interpreted the sexual difficulties as incompatibility and chosen to seek different partners rather than healing the real issue. But in time the pattern would resurface. As it happened, enough safety was present between them that a healing crisis was invoked. Will had unconsciously picked up on Chandra's resistance to lovemaking, as well as her unresolved shame and guilt, and mirrored it back to her with his loss of desire. His response then became a catalyst for the initial discovery of Chandra's wound.

The longer Chandra blamed Will for their predicament, the longer she avoided the real source of her pain. Blame is a powerful and ruthless defense against facing one's self in the moment. When we are able to bring our attention to the moment, facing into our deepest feelings, healing ensues at the appropriate pace. Again, reactive patterns rooted in the past cannot survive the Now.

Once Chandra got in touch with the shame, it shifted, and a profoundly wounded, angry voice inside her began to surface. This was the next level of her healing. She found a voice of extraordinary outrage at being violated and finally began to honor that place within herself that wanted absolutely nothing to do with men at this point in her life. At this moment, though angry, Chandra no longer held Will responsible for the loss of sexual interest. She saw that he was giving voice to her own wounded, troubled, inner psyche. Sexual intimacy was the last thing on Chandra's mind at this point in their recovery. Each time Chandra tried to make love she was confronted with the face of her stepfather.

As Chandra rode out the waves of anger, it gradually shifted to a deep ache in her heart. Periodically she would have a great flurry of thoughts and insights concerning her relationships over the years. But spiritual healing required her to relinquish all concepts and to instead move deeper into the ache in her heart. Rather than act out the pain through angry outbursts toward Will, we encouraged Chandra to contain it. It was at this point that a sense of terror began to surface as Chandra allowed herself to experience the wound caused by her stepfather's sexual abuse of her.

The skill in emotional healing is not to interfere through unnecessary analysis, but rather to allow focused attention to cut through deeper and deeper layers of feeling. We do this by staying present for whatever feelings arise.

Over the next difficult year, Will and Chandra experienced a range of emotions and engaged in much self-disclosure and self-revelation. At times it was extraordinarily painful. Out of fear, they would periodically move back into their heads, trying to logically resolve the discomforts arising between them. Inevitably, they would have to surrender to the feelings that sought acknowledgment and expression before rational thinking and resolution could occur. Increasingly, Chandra began accessing a deep, inner part of herself that had never been abused, that felt strong, self-sufficient, and whole. She came to recognize this as her essence, her spiritual core.

Chandra's healing was a positive catalyst for Will's, reawakening in him the unfinished business of his own childhood. Will was the model of control: soft voice, perfect dress, his day planner filled up to the minute for each week. But had he left any time for intimacy? Why the fear of spontaneity, of letting go of control? Indeed, Chandra's process of self-discovery was so intense that Will was now forced to feel emotions that he had spent an entire adult life trying desperately to avoid. Her anger was a catalyst.

Beneath the gentle, well-mannered exterior of this man was someone deeply troubled over the unresolved issues of his own childhood. Now in the spotlight of Chandra's ruthless honesty, it was becoming increasingly difficult to deny his own suppressed emotions. Will's parents had kept a tight rein on emotional expression. Any type of emotional outburst was strictly forbidden. Like all children, Will craved approval from his parents and therefore learned to suppress his feelings in order to please them. In this way, he grew up feeling afraid of his emotions. His social mask was charming and cordial, but inside he was frightened, tense, and angry. Prior to Chandra's healing work, Will was not only completely out of touch with his anger, he was unable to cry when he was sad or admit fear when he was afraid.

Will's calm, pleasing persona was a strategy developed over many years for manipulating people into satisfying his needs for emotional safety and approval. Until now it seemed to work quite well, though it had little to do with authentic love. Chandra's real gift to Will was her honesty and the refusal to allow his needs to control her. His initial response was one of anger toward Chandra for no longer satisfying his apparent needs. But over time Chandra's refusal to move off her center forced Will to reflect deeper into the shadowy spaces of his own heart. The nice-guy persona was showing some serious cracks. His anger went way beyond his marriage; it was rooted in countless childhood situations when he had been upset but couldn't show it, when he was sad but couldn't cry.

Will was disturbed at times by the fact that much of his healing was happening from his gut, (the seat of much anger) and that he didn't feel his heart was opening. But we reassured him of their connection; that you cannot open your heart and at the same time hold on to past resentments and judgments in a tight belly. He slowly developed faith in his capacity to open to deep feelings and heavy states of mind like fear, anger, and rage.

At times Will was encouraged to fully express his pain. It was all right to get angry, yell, and cry. At other times he was encouraged to contain it. That is, he neither acted out the emotion nor suppressed it. He simply remained present for it. In this way his awareness was drawn to deeper and deeper layers of unguarded feeling. He was getting at the root of his emotional reactivity. His heart was opening to embrace his shadow, all the parts of himself that he had rejected and repressed growing up.

The key in this kind of healing is to lean directly into our discomfort. The pain becomes a way into the essence of the heart, which is never wounded by pain. In welcoming anger, for instance, we get in touch with the enormous healing energy stored behind the anger. In becoming aware of our fear— its naked quality—we make contact with the enormous healing energy that resides beyond it.

As adults we have access to emotional and psychological resources that we didn't have as children. By consciously reentering the territory of our previous wounds, we discover a new potential for healing. We are also able to uncover and evaluate our core patterns from a more mature perspective.

It is important to remember that our emotional patterns, including our defenses, evolved from events that overwhelmed us. Such events generate more energy in us than we are able to release and thus get stored in the subconscious. We learn to avoid anything that re-stimulates memory of the original painful experience. It now becomes clear why we often resist deep intimacy. To become truly intimate we have to undress our most tender wounds.

This process is the disillusionment we all go through in our relationships. Our healing takes a downward turn at this point, because it involves our shadow work. Will was learning, in the only way one can, that true intimacy is no hiding place for our pain; that, in fact, in love there is no hiding place for the ego at all. We become naked. In the ashes of our love we deconstruct the faulty notions of a wounded and separate self. In so doing, we often encounter the fierce Kali aspect of truth. Kali is an Indian archetype known for dismantling the ego. This is actually the deeper part of us that is unwilling to compromise our clarity. Eventually we can find ourselves in a still space behind the wound of anger, self-righteousness, submissiveness, dominance, and all the various strategies of our cracked identities.

As the heart breaks open through inquiry, we come to the realization that the Invisible Wedding is not really about the other. It's about the Self. Love at this depth is a potent challenge to our self-concepts as deeply held patterns of fear and survival are uprooted by the torch of our awareness and confession. Love dismantles us. We unmask. We become transparent.

Will came to the precious insight that whatever truth was gained in his relationship to Chandra came from the ashes of his own transformation. He saw that she was neither responsible for his happiness nor his pain. He could not look toward her for consolation. Will's attention shifted to his own spiritual core. The inner journey was sparked. In the healing of his own heart, Will discovered a greater capacity to be present for Chandra.

As we go within we become aware of our profound interconnectedness. The heart stripped of its defenses becomes strong, tender, and transparent. Finally, we realize there is only one heart. Conflict dissolves in the absence of separation. The circle that contains us individually opens to include each other. The circle that opens to each other eventually comes to embrace life in a bigger way.

PHYSICAL SENSATIONS: MESSAGES TO OURSELVES

The starting point for real communication is always within our own body. How can we communicate clearly with another without first listening to ourselves? We can begin with an awareness of sensation. Our bodies are constantly sending out messages. What is our belly trying to tell us by its chronic tension? By its butterflies? What is our throat trying to communicate when it becomes difficult to talk or swallow? What is our chest communicating with our inability to breathe freely and unrestricted? What does the chronic pain in our middle back have to teach us about love or fear in the heart, and our need to forgive? What resentments are we unable to let go of in the tightness of our colon?

Chandra had surgery for a degenerated disc in her neck, behind her throat. Was there a connection behind keeping her mouth shut about her abuse and the loss of movement in her vertebrae? There is always at some level a mind/body connection.

We instructed Will and Chandra to meditate on physical sensations to complement their deep emotional work. We began by simply having them close their eyes and place their attention on various parts of the body for ten minutes, morning and evening. This helped sensitize them to their feelings and encouraged them to recognize the intimate relationship between mental states and their physiology. In this way they learned experientially about the intimate relationship between thought and chemistry. Fearful thoughts tend to produce tightness around the chest and shoulders. Anger often produces tension in the belly and back. Joy relaxes the body. With greater awareness we come to see that the slightest fluctuation of thought or feeling has a corresponding physiological reaction. This subtle relationship between our mind and body is the invisible basis of our relationship with each other. Unacknowledged tensions inside us will eventually get acted out between us, underscoring the very practical benefit of daily self-investigation.

Together, as they continued opening, Will and Chandra's awareness penetrated into increasingly subtle levels of feeling. Old wounds periodically arose and were let go. Meditating on sensation was a perfect complement to the emotional work they were doing with one another; each aspect supported the other in the overall process of inner work. Eventually they learned to interpret conflict that surfaced as just another opportunity for further exploration, for the heart to open up. Tension indicated a need to investigate the subtle relationship between heart and mind, and the distance between a separate me and you.

When Will and Chandra felt stressed in their communication they learned to tune into the sensations floating in their bodies, and to translate them into meaningful dialogue as a starting point for sharing. This was not always an easy or comfortable process; but when they stuck with it, the sensations eventually yielded to insight and relaxation. This brought them immediately into the vast resourcefulness of the present moment.

In the dismantling of conflict we eventually come to these questions: Who are we actually fighting against? What is the real source of our conflict? Is it our partners? Is it our parents? Or is it perhaps the false sense of separateness reinforced by traumatic events of our pasts? Who and what lies behind these masks, these cracked identities? In posing such questions, we move from the surface level of argument to a deep level of self-inquiry. Such questions arise from the depths. The momentum of conflict, the energy in the storm, can lead us to address the issue of conflict at its very root. It is for this reason that we strongly advocate the welcoming of conflict as it arises in the moment. What better moment to investigate the foundation and structure of the ego than in the heat of conflict? There can be no true resolution of conflict without addressing the basic nature of the ego and the core beliefs that reinforce our separateness.

Over the years, we are drawn back time and again to the realization that our primary relationship is always with ourselves. Our relationship is a reflection of the delicate ebb and flow of attention between our own hearts and minds. On the path of love we learn to listen to the highly sensitive patterns of breath, heartbeat, thought, and feeling. The distance between our partner and us is on the same line that lies between our own heads and hearts; or, we can say it is the same distance that lies between us and our Beloved.

Leonard Orr, an old friend and founder of the Rebirthing movement (a powerful form of breath work and deep healing), once told me (David) that the best way to heal a broken heart is to let it break. Think about it: We spend enormous amounts of time and energy simply trying to avoid getting hurt. To avoid the blow of the heart breaking open to its original pain, we compensate with false pride, detachment, judgment, approval-seeking and anger. We unconsciously avoid restimulation of our first wounds and then lament the loneliness and lack of intimacy in our lives. What we experience as heartbreak is actually the painful dissolution of our defenses surrounding our capacity for love. When we can embrace the heartbreak, it allows us to open. *The Invisible Wedding* is about willingly and consciously opening ourselves to reveal our naked heart. Gradually, we think, speak, and act from our deeper essence, and our lives come to reflect greater wholeness.

A simple way to become aware of our feelings so that we can move toward wholeness is to begin to notice the sensations in our bodies. Notice the fluctuating bodily sensations as you discuss various issues together. How does it feel in your chest when your partner brings up a woman's name from a past relationship? How does it feel in your body when your partner criticizes you in front of your children or friends? Do your shoulders tighten? Does your stomach contract? How does it feel when your partner is emotionally unavailable and refuses valid feedback? Pierce into that feeling with the sword of attention. Attention dissolves fear.

Feeling the sensation of anger—a knot in the stomach or tension in the chest—can lead us into a deeper appreciation of the present. Many people believe anger to be a primary feeling. Yet when we are able to truly experience our anger internally, by containing it rather than suppressing it or projecting it immediately out onto our partner, we become aware that underneath the anger is the sense of being hurt. Feeling our hurt, as difficult as this can be at times, is a doorway into deeper realms of the heart. From where did this hurt initially arise? Somewhere, sometime, fear and the feeling of not being loved overwhelmed us. Once we touch the essential feeling of being unloved in present time, the pain yields, love returns, and tremendous energy is released. The root feeling of fear dissolves into love, in the spacious awareness of the present moment.

Pain is a message to return to the sense of being loved. Fear is an indicator of our need to remember our wholeness. This sense of being held in the arms of love arises as we turn within, welcoming in both intense pleasure and pain with our awareness.

As Chandra and Will opened to the pain surrounding the memories of past abuses, they discovered new and richer territories of emotional intimacy. They discovered that at the level of essence, they were not their stories. Their sexual relationship took on new depth, filled with heart, unrestricted passion, and freedom. Pain and conflict were simply messengers indicating the need to self-investigate. They ceased relying on one another for the meeting of their deepest needs and instead turned their attention inward toward their own wholeness. What began as a conventional fear-based relationship evolved into a true spiritual partnership that shunned nothing and placed everything between them at the feet of the Beloved.

THE ABANDONMENT PATTERN

Having experienced the trauma of severe loss, many people run like wild horses from committed relationships. Sometimes such loss cuts so deep into the soft muscle of the heart that we never fully reveal ourselves again. How we compensate varies. Some find partners but still manage to stay aloof and hidden. Some become exceptionally easy-going and non-confrontive, suppressing any show of anger in an attempt to win approval and acceptance. Others become fiercely independent (in or out of relationship), avoiding any hint of dependency and vulnerability.

In each case, a wall is set firmly around the heart; like a moat it refuses entry into the vulnerable territory of authentic human contact and connection.

We once counseled a woman named Amy who had been adopted as a young child. She was involved in healing a terrible bout of systemic candida. We found it interesting that the candida kicked in at exactly the point when her partner abandoned her for someone else. Amy fell apart and was hardly able to work or function any longer in the world. Having faced long-term illness ourselves, we knew that chronic physical patterns are often symptoms for deeper emotional wounds. We approached her from this perspective, although she often resisted our pointing to deeper emotional issues.

Slowly, over many months of working together, Amy peeled back the layers of pain and fear that stood between her body's symptoms and the deep underlying trauma of having lost her parents as a baby, and the resulting adoption. Before each breakthrough into new feeling, her symptoms of fatigue and irritability would increase dramatically. Once she finally was able to acknowledge the underlying emotions, the symptoms began to lighten. And what were the feelings that surfaced? Anxiety. Terror. Rage. Sadness. Despair. A sense of emptiness. As her attention deepened, Amy learned to contain what she described as "an endless ocean of grief." She found these emotions so frightening that she had never before been able to relax completely with another person. Beneath the tension loomed the core belief that one day every relationship would end in abandonment. Etched in the delicate fibers of Amy's heart was the mental imperative that love equates with unbearable loss.

Unable to acknowledge her core belief around abandonment and feel fully the accompanying emotional trauma, Amy had indeed manifested her worst fears over and over. Although she claimed that the therapy sessions were causing distress, she eventually acknowledged that the pain she felt was the catalyst for feelings she had bottled up inside since birth. She was undressing the heart. At times she ranted and cried. At other times she sat completely still with eyes closed, inviting into her awareness whatever thoughts and feelings wanted to surface.

The value of containing our experience—neither suppressing nor expressing—is that it allows our awareness to dive deeply to the root of the problem. The undischarged energy behind the tension allows us to cut through resistance and make contact with the original wound. Once we openly encounter the original wound the blocked energy is released. The mind/body relaxes, and a profound sense of being held in love returns. But we must be able to become aware of and contain a profound level of pain.

After a year of intense therapy, Amy's systemic candida was nearly healed. She was dating but had not yet connected with someone with whom she wanted to be intimate. Getting involved in an intimate relationship would certainly be an acid test as to the extent of her healing. Time will tell.

Sometimes a wound must be retraumatized in order for our minds and bodies to once again link up to it on the level of feeling. For Amy, the childhood pain of abandonment was so excruciating that her attention separated from it out of her need for survival. It remained repressed until she experienced another abandonment of sufficient intensity to reawaken the original pain. The loss of her relationship became a catalyst for accessing the original wound.

The following is another abandonment story. It involves a couple we will call the Medusa and the Ice Man.

THE MEDUSA AND THE ICEMAN

While first sitting with Roger and his wife, Kathy, we were struck by their sense of apparent control. Every type of conflict or disagreement was handled completely logically, in the head. Both were college professors and had learned to think out their feelings with articulate explanations.

Why were they in therapy? Their marriage had become flat, passionless, they explained. They were at a serious impasse and sought help in resolving it. It seems Roger would completely immerse himself in his work until finally Kathy would explode in a barrage of criticism and complaint. Roger would briefly come out of his shell only to resume the pattern once the pressure was off. In the last couple years Kathy had practically given up, and the distance between them had grown.

Each time Kathy tried to communicate on a feeling level Roger would move immediately into his head, digging up some justification for his or her speech or behavior. We had confronted this many times before in both ourselves and other clients for whom painful feelings were denied. We had ourselves unconsciously shifted into our minds as a way of avoiding heartache. We finally suggested that instead of trying to match Roger's mind, Kathy practice staying present for her feelings. That little bit of advice was the flint that finally created enough friction between them to get a real fire going.

As she got in touch with the intensity of her pain, Kathy began belting out statements like, "I'm sick to death of being shut out all the time" . . . "It makes me angry when you disappear into your head." She was enraged at Roger's detachment, finally confessing her loneliness in living with an Ice Man unable or unwilling to express real warmth and affection. Now the Ice Man was face to face with Medusa.

Roger's habitual response was to move deeper into his head for protection. We suggested that this time Kathy contain her wrath and find the Iceman within herself. At that moment, as Roger relaxed, we asked him if he could locate a sensation in his body. He acknowledged that he felt tension in his chest. Suggesting at this point that Roger close his eyes, we guided him to breathe deeply up into his heart. His face started tightening up, and small tears appeared in the corners of his eyes. Roger could no longer contain his pain as he cried out his sorrow and guilt for emotionally abandoning his wife and two children. Kathy's face visibly softened. For the first time in many years they began to actually hear each other's pain. The pain felt as deep and wide as the Grand Canyon.

When Roger was finished, Kathy expressed without blame or criticism the honest pain, frustration, and sheer loneliness of living with such little emotion or affection for so many years. Her eyes, red with tears, were finally seeing deep into the one heart between them. She expressed the need for Roger to really listen without becoming defensive. She needed his unguarded presence. For Roger, this meant he would have to learn to listen from his heart, not his head. He would have to learn to embrace the pain as it arose, instead of denying it by projecting it onto his wife. Kathy finally had his full attention; Roger was front and center. In the following weeks each told their stories.

Roger had lost his father when he was five. Unable to deal emotionally with the grief, he cultivated an academic mind for escape and protection. The trauma remained buried within. Staying in his head was a way to avoid the terrible insecurity of feeling abandoned. It was also a protection against feeling the anger. As Roger matured he took refuge not in people but in books, magazines, newspapers, television, career, and intellectual thought. The risk of real intimacy was extraordinarily high. The child inside the man did not feel he could endure another major loss; thus, Roger remained aloof from the people he loved most. In the past, one relationship after another ended in the woman's upset and rage at his lack of presence. Now, for the first time, the wall was coming down. Roger was like a skinned snake coming out of the thicket of his defenses.

In Roger's mind, love meant unbearable loss. His fear of abandonment was the thread that held together his false identity as the Ice Man. It was finally unraveling.

It took many months for Roger to trust his heart and re-verse the tendency to move into his mind. His head was his stable place of refuge against deep human contact and the pos-sibility of feeling grief. When emotionally threatened, Roger would suddenly erect the wall, turning again into the cold, cal-culating, Ice Man. Kathy's Medusa, in part a reflection of Roger's suppressed anger, would resurface with a vengeance, but it would not last long. Self-investigation invariably re-vealed the defenses they had erected. Each time they made contact with real feeling, the crack in their armor widened a little more. As Roger got in touch with his anger, and the oc-casional need to express it, Kathy no longer felt enraged. They experienced a deepening presence—an essence—that they had not connected to since first falling in love.

Walls grow over time. Gradually, unconsciously, they are raised and reinforced by repeated experiences. In the same way, they tend to fall slowly. Each time Roger and Kathy were able to lower their defenses by remaining unguarded, the more willing and trusting they became to live without them. They learned to stay present, listen, and move together into their hearts. They learned to recognize resistance. Withdrawing eye contact and affection, needing to be right, staying compul-sively busy, rationalizing their feelings, each of these behaviors indicated a need to relax into feeling.

Kathy had her own past issues to work through. Although she had not had to endure the physical loss of a parent as a child, she had been emotionally abandoned by an alcoholic mother and a powerful, dominating father who emotionally distanced himself from his family. Kathy had repeatedly promised herself that she would never marry someone like him, yet this was the only type of male her subconscious rec-ognized. The angry Medusa archetype was born, in part, from the pain of projecting her feminine power onto a male (her father). It was also fed by a lifetime of unmet emotional needs for affection and support.

Kathy's self-worth had taken a beating from both sides. She felt invalidated by her mother and rejected by her father. By peeling back the emotional armor of her defenses, by leaning into her discomfort and resisting the tendency to blame Roger, she began to access this undischarged pain of her childhood. This is the healing edge. Kathy took the attention off her husband and faced herself. To the mind this transformation is a virtual death. In touching our pain we simultaneously face the core beliefs that apparently supported our survival all these years. In Kathy's case, these beliefs included: He can't really love me, No man can be trusted, and I need his approval to feel safe. Such beliefs begin to surface and finally collapse in the light of self-investigation. Kathy faced her inner feelings of unworthiness and fear to a degree she had never before experienced because she was no longer able to side-step them through blame. At times she was overwhelmed. But the gift of such self-investigation is priceless. Kathy finally began to reclaim the power she had given over to her father forty years ago.

As we grow in the ability to contain and absorb whatever hidden material arises in our awareness, we begin to access the undiluted, unconditioned essence that shines at the core of our nature. Touching essence is always accompanied by a strong sense of wholeness and is independent of whatever conditions might be present around us. We do not arrive at essence by analysis but by the acceptance of what is. We simply turn and face ourselves.

Once Kathy was able to embrace her pain and experience her essence—beyond her identity as wife, daughter, college professor—she naturally felt a deeper compassion for her

partner's predicament. Now she could be present for him because she was present for herself. Roger had been, in part, a
mirror of her inner Ice Man; just as she was, in part, a reflection of the imaginary Medusa inside Roger.

Through the mirror of their relationship Kathy and Roger
began an intense and dramatic process of healing. It was a rebirth of feeling and an opening of their hearts, which had been
closed since early childhood. The unacknowledged pattern of
abandonment that had played such a crucial part in both their
lives had very nearly capsized the ship of their relationship.

It is important to emphasize that the abandonment pattern
does not have to involve the physical departure of someone close
to us. We can feel abandoned at not being honored for our gifts
as a child. We can feel emotionally abandoned by parents, siblings, or close friends who for whatever reason were unable to
meet our needs. Some children whose parents work many hours
each day grow up feeling abandoned and therefore frightened at
the notion of real intimacy. An adolescent girl who opens up to
her partner sexually and is then rejected might carry the wound
of that experience into adulthood if she doesn't find the guidance
and support needed to heal. Children of alcoholics frequently
grow up with terrible feelings of abandonment and rejection because their parents consistently acted out their addiction to alcohol rather than attend to the needs of their children.

The fear of abandonment can manifest at any time in a long
term relationship. Even twenty years down the path we can
find ourselves trying to hide from deepening intimacy. Affairs
are, in certain cases, a way of masking our fear of loss. Chronic
illness is also often related to abandonment issues. After working with hundreds of individuals and couples, it is clear to us
that the fear of abandonment is at the emotional heart of many

conflicts and is rooted in the most primary levels of the sub-conscious. It appears that early on in the development of the ego we experience ourselves as increasingly separate from the unified Web of Life. This corresponds to a subtle shift in awareness from the feeling nature of the heart into the analytical nature of the mind. A sense, however imperceptible, arises that we are separate from the Whole. From this mistake of the intellect—as it is referred to in Eastern wisdom—the feeling of being unloved grows in our awareness.

Many personality quirks evolve to compensate for our hidden insecurity. And subsequent experiences of loss and betrayal serve to further reinforce the idea that we are separate. Many people unconsciously avoid intimacy because of the faintest imprint of our first divorce from life itself. We subconsciously fear abandonment. This discomfort consistently points out the need to return to the Beloved, to the One inside that embodies unconditional love beyond the faulty perception of the mind. It is only in our return to the heart that we come to realize the lie of the mind, the idea that we could ever be separate from the One, the Whole. All abandonment issues get resolved here in our essence, in the full remembrance of our wholeness.

SEEING FROM THE HEART

No matter how difficult our life situation, from the wider perspective of the Beloved everything is unfolding exactly as it must. There is no room for error in a universe of infinite correlation. Abandonment, betrayal, abuse, all can be powerful catalysts for finding the true and infinite source of love within.

This is a painful concept for the ego to accept, especially in the West. We pride ourselves on being independent and in control. The mind lives in the black and white realm of duality. But once we view life as an incomprehensible mystery, one in which everything is unfolding according to plan, a deep relaxation dawns and life becomes playful and full of surprises.

Once we're fully present we realize that in essence we are that love that we had been seeking outside. Here in the present moment we realize that no matter what our circumstances are or were in the past we are basically, fundamentally, loved. The present moment is spacious. There's room in this moment for tears, unbearable pain and longing, the sadness of loss or abandonment, and the calling out for mercy. It is here in the raw and direct perception of what is that all conflict ends. It is resolved in love, in the exquisite paradox of being separate yet one in heart. This is the Naked Heart of a Rumi, Hafiz, Mother Theresa, all of us.

Most people have at least fleetingly experienced the sense of everything falling into place. Moments when the veil of separateness seems to lift and we find ourselves suddenly free from the self-conscious restraints of ego-consciousness. Such moments affirm the basic unity underlying the seeming separateness, chaos and turmoil of ordinary life. From this vantage point, animals, trees, a stranger's face, even a pile of garbage all seem to whisper some basic design. We are simply seeing from the heart, through the eyes of the Beloved. Such moments of profound innocence, of seeing into the unity of things, affirm that we are threads in a vast, utterly incomprehensible Web of Life. Everything is complete in the moment. There is something deeply satisfying in the intuitive knowing that we are part of a large ensemble cast that includes the entire universe! Now, are we the Dancer . . . or the danced?

CHAPTER THREE

First Impressions

There's no cure, except the retreat into love,
for the suffering of subtly afflicted hearts.
—RUMI

Many of the dynamics we experience in our spiritual partnerships have their roots in our family of origin. Our childhood home is our first school, and our parents are our first relationship teachers. Like a good Zen master, their mode of teaching is often not what they specifically tell us about relating, but how they live it on a daily basis. As children, we watch and internalize the behavior of our parents based upon our interpretation of what we see happening around us. For this reason, most of us who want to become conscious of the powerful, underlying forces at work in our lives and intimate relationships will make the journey back into childhood to revisit our early experiences.

Traditional spiritual practices like meditation, prayer, and yoga, though important aspects of healing are not always adequate for releasing the debilitating primal wounds incurred in childhood. To navigate our way through life and our relationships, we need a clear understanding of our family of origin's pattern of relating, as well as the programming we received when we were young.

BASIC GOODNESS

Many of us who have taken various paths to enlightenment have found ourselves having to investigate our Western culture and our families as part of our quest. It is not always an easy passage. As we mature it can be humbling—and healing—to accept that we may not be able to change all the programming we received in our families, even though we're aware of it. As well, too much analysis of our past can result in our feeling flawed. This is because the ego attaches itself to negative experiences of the past (bad parenting, schooling, etc.) to justify the avoidance of relationship in the present. A challenge arises: Can we skillfully investigate our psychological roots without ending up feeling defective?

We can . . . if we take one small step beyond the ego and sense that, in the moment, life feels remarkably sane, integrated, and whole. We can come to understand that there is a basic goodness to life, a kind of fundamental perfection at the heart of everything. Traumatic childhoods, messy relationships, bad teachers, suffering and pain, all fit into a fundamental—if inexplicable—pattern. When we view our family history from this wider perspective, there is nobody to blame, not even bad parents.

There is a remarkable passage in the spiritual classic *I Am That*, when the sage, Nisaragadatta Maharaj, says in a dialogue with a student:

> For anything to happen, the entire universe must coincide.
> It is wrong to believe that anything in particular can
> cause an event.

How does this relate to our childhood? What happened in the past, happened because it had to. When we remove blame and judgment from our life equation, we remove the thought that we—or anybody—are fundamentally flawed. From the ego-transcended view of our essence and the Beloved, everything simply is as it is, free of judgment and fear. This does not mean that we avoid looking at difficult issues that might arise. It is not an excuse to remain blind. A superficial understanding of basic goodness can be used to justify denial and passive or negative behavior, and to avoid facing the full impact of painful events. The intent here is just the opposite. Accepting the idea of basic goodness allows us to investigate our conditioning free from the sense of wrongdoing and blame. It provides a neutral context to evaluate our pasts without reinforcing the already tenacious emotional attachment to our personal story.

In the journey inward many discover that a wound, once fully welcomed, becomes a doorway out of the ego and into the heart, a way into the recognition of our intrinsic wholeness. Viewing our lives from this perspective, nothing is out of place. We realize that without the wounding we would not have gained our present understanding. Gratitude replaces the sense of being flawed. Acceptance replaces judgment and the need for punishment.

THE WOUNDING

No one gets through childhood without getting wounded; it's part of the curriculum. We may have been invalidated with statements like: "You should be ashamed of yourself!" or

"Stop your silly crying! You have no reason to feel that way!" Perhaps our trust was subtly violated each time we experienced the incongruity of our parent's words and their behavior. Or maybe our hearts were silently broken each time our parents withheld their love from us out of anger or punishment. In cases of sexual abuse the wounds branch out from the genitals and groin, up to the heart and then out into the vast world of our relationships.

Like Jesus nailed to the cross, children are often crucified by the unexamined fear of and pain brought on by the adults they love. The cultivation of intimacy both with oneself and others can require a careful, merciful, unraveling and mending of these wounds. We cannot deny our personal history and expect to find intimacy with another. When we do deny it, the unresolved traumas from our childhood return to haunt us like ghosts.

Each time our trust is betrayed as children, each time we are harshly criticized, each time our feelings are violated through shame or excessive punishment and we are unable to release the tension, like a turtle pulling its neck in for protection, our hearts contract. We leap into our conceptual minds for protection. As we mature our identity as isolated untrusting individuals solidifies. Reactive emotional patterns stitched together by anger, denial, projection, false pride, arrogance, odd sexual proclivities and various fight or flight responses become compensatory strategies, arising in an effort to avoid the unresolved pain of the initial childhood experience. These patterns come to define us, making up the fabric of our false identity, or ego. In essence, the dark inner shadow that compels our neurotic behavior is comprised of the unresolved pain, anger, fear and feelings of impotence left over from earlier experiences. For many of us, our pain-filled shadows continue to grow as we get older.

Once back in the eighties, I (David) was having breakfast with a friend in the Haight district of San Francisco. Glancing out the window I noticed a young couple crossing the street. They were punks, dressed in black leather, chains, boots and dark, heavy make-up. As they drew near, I caught the young man's pale, blue eyes and for a moment saw beyond the smoke of his persona. What I witnessed was a thin, tender young soul trying desperately to hide his fear and vulnerability.

Turning to my companion I asked what she thought of the whole youth scene. She was older than I, in her mid-fifties at the time, and said, "These kids are a manifestation of our crazy world today, David. Our planet is post-Hiroshima. My God, these kids are scared to death!" She was right, of course. Young people are walking, breathing, living antennae, vibrating to the mad, chaotic culture in which we live.

A young child sees, hears, touches, tastes, smells, and feels at magnified quantum depths. In a child's fresh consciousness no veil can mask the secrets of those around her. In early childhood, perception is still subtle, unclouded, unconditioned. A child feels intuitively the emotional energies in the household. She picks up on a subtle gesture, a held breath, a furrowed brow or an unspoken word. By the age of three or four a child has a basic blueprint of how life works, how men and women act and interact. Already her family's core beliefs about the body, sexuality, gender, God, and relating have been imprinted. This material becomes her personal storyline forming her identity as a separate, autonomous self. Her own life experiences will continue to reinforce—and at times modify—this conditioning.

Our parents are our first and most powerful relationship teachers. More than anyone else they help shape the unconscious ground and nurture the roots out of which all subsequent relationship dynamics arise. As adults, we tend to recreate an emotional climate in our homes similar to what we experienced as children, even when our current circumstances look completely different. Left unexamined, our intimate relationships will typically conform to the conditioning imprinted in our early childhood. A girl who is sexually abused by her father often learns to equate love with shame and disrespect. A young boy punished by physical beatings typically learns to equate pain with intimacy. A child who loses a parent through divorce or death and is unable to face and understand the experience often learns to equate love with loss. These patterns—and all the defensive posturing that attend them—often reemerge later in life as we attempt to enter the complex terrain of emotional intimacy.

THE MIRROR OF INTIMACY AND THE TRANSFORMATION OF CONFLICT

Intimacy, like a deep meditative practice, can be a potent challenge to our defenses. It mirrors our concepts and conflict about love and life. It begins to reflect the terrain of our subconscious. It highlights the knotted shapes and textures of our reactive patterns. Intimacy forces us to address in some way the gap between our head and heart and any feelings buried inside. Staying truly present at a feeling level and being deeply intimate go hand in hand. As we attempt to let each other into our hearts, we will often be pushed up against our deepest defenses in an effort to divert attention away from the re-stimulation of our pain bodies. And there will be times when we will want to run.

Sometimes we turn away in fear, which we disguise as blame. Or rush to our intellects for analysis and reasoning as the ego guards against disclosure. At other times our resistance gives way, allowing us to gain personal insight and to experience the gift of healing that comes through authentic unguarded intimacy.

Conflict releases a powerful energy that can then be used in our process of transformation. Depending on its intensity, conflict can cause our minds to conjure up a sense of chaos, loss of control, and violence. But in fact, conflict is a window into our selves. When we are in conflict our various fixations and survival strategies become greatly highlighted, creating a window of opportunity for learning and growth. We can ask ourselves, what unexamined hurt lies behind this rage? What old wound resides behind this deep sadness? What is the cause of this arrogance, and what hidden memory resides beneath it? Discovering the answers to such questions requires that we welcome in what's been rejected, that we remain present in the midst of our discomfort. More important than thinking about the causes of our pain is making contact with it, touching the emotional nerve. How many of us were guided as children to remain present and vulnerable for painful feelings? Unfortunately, too few of us witnessed our parents becoming vulnerable with each other through the chaos of conflict resolution. Too many of us learned instead to suppress our discomfort and to avoid resolving our problems at their root level.

Faye experienced an almost continuous underlying feeling of tension between her parents. She rarely saw them completely resolve the periodic disagreements that arose. Faye's mother would appear upset. Her father would placate, apologize, and

the disagreement would apparently be over. But was it? Or was
the tension simply buried temporarily beneath the growing
heap of past unresolved issues? In the heat of another argument,
old wounds resurfaced with a vengeance. Issues that supposedly
had been worked through previously would arise for another
round. Why? The core issues had never been totally, unconditionally, embraced and worked through. For Faye's family, conflict resolution meant suppression of feelings, and for many
years her parents lived with an underlying animosity, which
permeated the atmosphere of the family home.

What might have been passed on to the children as a result?
The relationship model Faye's parents projected was one of
tension. Everyone learned to live with it but never truly healed
from it. The children were taught to suppress disagreements
rather than risk the discomfort of confrontation. The parents
also projected limiting archetypes about men and women:
Mother was frustrated and chronically irritated; Father was
passive, an inadequate male who seemed never able to satisfy
his wife. Neither of these archetypes was an accurate picture
of their whole selves, but because they got stuck in these roles,
their communication also got stuck.

For children, the archetypes acted out by their parents form
a kind of inner portrait of male/female energy so that later we
tend to attract partners who conform or contrast in some fundamental way to that portrait. It is important to point out that
Faye's parents modeled many positive qualities as well. They
were generous, tolerant, and spiritually minded, and they gra-
ciously provided for their four children's upbringing and education. These factors also played a significant part in Faye's
conditioning.

Each child responds differently to the family dynamic. We take on different roles according to the needs of the family as a whole. Whereas one child might become rebellious, another might withdraw or become overly pleasing in an attempt to harmonize the parents. In Faye's case, she became the good child, outwardly pleasing but inwardly holding resentment toward males, much as her mother did. One of her emotional imprints or core beliefs ran something like this: *Males are inadequate and cannot be counted on.* Keep in mind that core beliefs are thoughts that get frozen around a particular theme or issue. They point to a particular mental pattern but do not define the whole person.

In the heat of an argument Faye would blast me with weeks of stored-up anger over various unresolved issues, as if trying to make me pay emotionally for every moment I had not lived up to her expectations. For several years it seemed that regardless of my own personal growth she continued to see me as a weak, incompetent male. Together, as we explored the pattern, it was evident she related to me much the way her mother had related toward her father. Continued open dialogue and the growing ability to remain unguarded finally allowed Faye to release me from the cross hairs of her past conditioning, though it required us to stay deeply present in the midst of chaos and emotional unease.

It was, of course, no accident that Faye happened to be attracted to me as a mate. In part her intuitive, unconscious perceptions resonated with something inside me; the archetype of the weak but angry male was just one of many figures alive and well in me. My father's alcoholism had been very potent in stripping away any consistent sense of masculine honor that might have tried to stabilize in my childhood home.

In the beginning I unconsciously accepted Faye's projection like a well-fitted shoe, though a part of me fought against it. From years of listening to my mother's bitter complaints, I knew well the voice of feminine hostility. That particular feminine archetype had also become a part of me, and was now being given a voice through Faye. It was as if she became an instrument for my own subconscious. Such are the gifts and challenges of intimate relationships. We mirror the aspects in us that got rejected. Eventually I came to appreciate Faye as a mirror of my pain, rather than the source. Reaching this insight enabled our healing agenda to advance.

Once we acknowledge that our partner is a reflection of that which we deny, conflict quickly shifts to an opportunity. Conflict becomes a highly creative force that helps us to face and release unresolved issues of our pasts. We do this by getting to the point of welcoming feedback—whatever its content—without defense and unconditionally accepting our partners as they are. As we open inwardly to that which we previously denied, the apparent separation between us dissolves.

I heard a Buddhist teacher say that when the mind is quiet the heart speaks. In Christianity we are instructed to be still, and in that stillness experience God, or the Beloved. But this deepening of awareness—of presence—cannot happen without the willingness to directly experience pain as part of the process. And in the process of our heart opening, there is significant pain.

As the healing journey continued for us, Faye eventually got in touch with the place inside her that felt inadequate. Quite naturally, she began extending kindness rather than criticism toward me. For my part, I saw that Faye, in her costume of resentment, was a reflection of my own unloved self in need of contact. Once we were able to perceive our own basic goodness, it was easy to perceive it in each other. In our willingness to touch the real pain, to investigate beneath the fixed reflexes of our habitual patterns, we discovered a doorway to the Beloved, to the love inside that is the source of real intimacy. As defenses dropped we recovered the simple, subtle feeling of being loved. This feeling is independent of an other. It is part of our essence.

When we acknowledge our inherited patterns of unhealthy relating and accept the part of us that we previously rejected, we discover a sense of wholeness. An aspect of our psyche that was rejected returns home to the heart. We no longer find ourselves caught up in power struggles in which we act out—often violently—each other's unconscious patterns. The mind gradually surrenders its separateness to the underlying unity of an unguarded heart.

That which we find intolerable in others is that which we cannot face about ourselves. Once we fully accept this principle, our attention will turn inward automatically, and the painful emotional entanglements between us will begin to subside. We'll have more to share about projection in Chapter Four.

In an intimate relationship, conflict inevitably arises when our psychological defenses begin to dissolve, forcing suppressed feelings and past wounds to surface as part of the healing process. Something our partner may say or do might resonate with an unresolved situation from our past, causing our heart to contract once more. But such conflict can be used creatively when we embrace it and allow it to be investigated. Conflict resolution brings a renewed sense of harmony, intimacy, and emotional freedom into the relationship and family structure as a whole. It happens with our willingness to consider and touch whatever pain from the past might be present in the moment.

It is perfectly healthy to get into arguments. In fact, we need to blow off emotional steam and would not want to suppress our emotions. But we must learn to be reflective and to acknowledge that conflict is always an issue of the heart.

CONFLICT RESOLUTION: WHAT ARE YOUR FAMILY PATTERNS AND CORE BELIEFS?

It is beneficial for couples to ask themselves how they may have been programmed to respond to conflict. How might you and your partner respond to the following questions?

- What were some of the unresolved issues in our families of origin?
- How did our parents approach disagreements?
- Was it safe to express ourselves with regard to unpleasant issues?
- What roles did we find ourselves playing out in our childhood family? (The rebel? The quiet one? The peace keeper?)
- Are we still acting out the same basic roles today?
- Does each of us feel safe enough to touch our pain? Our partner's?
- Have we forgiven our parents for inadequate teachings regarding conflict resolution?

- What are our primary defense mechanisms? Denial, blame, arrogance, pride, anger?

Following are some common core beliefs. Which of these have you inherited from your family of origin?

- Conflict means he doesn't love me.
- Anger means I don't love him.
- Anger is not safe.
- Loving people don't fight.
- Spiritual people don't get angry.
- Conflict ends in loss.
- I deserve to be punished for negative thoughts and behaviors.

When we stumble into an emotional pattern and an accompanying core belief, we can begin to unravel it by bringing our awareness directly into the experience. We can lean into our discomfort and resist the tendency to blame our partner or intellectualize the problem. We can open to the pain—feel its naked quality—both in ourselves and the relationship. And we can ask ourselves, "How does it feel in my body at this moment? What is it about my partner's behavior that upsets or irritates me? How does this make me feel? Have I ever felt this way before—perhaps in my childhood?" By remaining unguarded in the midst of emotional pain, by staying in touch with our pain and our partner's, we can begin to dissolve our unwanted emotional pattern at its root. When we do so, the heart's capacity for love increases.

When we focus our awareness on any feeling we might have, we are eventually led to a deeper quality of love and acceptance. When we give our attention fully to our reactions in the moment, we come to recognize that love is at the basis of all feeling. But we can only do so unguarded, undefended, naked—without blame and without projecting our fears onto others.

MEN, WOMEN, AND HEART LESSONS

We walked into a supermarket last week catching the eye of a scruffy red-headed young boy, maybe seven years old, with a trail of tears running down his soft, pink cheeks. Suddenly a stressed mother grabbed him by his shirt collar, reprimanded him for crying, and dragged him out of the store. What might have been imprinted in this young boy's mind at that moment? *Don't cry. Submit to authority. You have to suppress your feelings in order to be loved. To feel too much is unsafe. It hurts too much to love.*

Like a vast underground river, feelings run deep beneath the surface of life. How many of us were guided to accept and embrace our vast feeling natures? Did our parents, teachers, and culture encourage us to experience our feelings, our tears, fears, laughter, and grief? Was anger a safe emotion? Or were we given the message, either covertly or overtly, that certain emotions were inappropriate, childish, dangerous, or wrong? Many people are ashamed of what they naturally feel, and all such conditioning influences our capacity for love as we enter the arena of intimate relating.

Males are often programmed to mask their feelings, to be tough. As boys we are unconsciously trained to desensitize ourselves to physical and emotional pain. Due to centuries of patriarchy invested in warfare, competition, and domination, such desensitization was a necessity. Unlike indigenous tribesman, the ancient Samurai of Japan and the Kashatriya of India who were taught to soften rather than to tense in battle, warriors in Western culture were not trained to be soft and relaxed in their bellies. And young males are still given the message to tighten their bellies, their vulnerable feeling centers, to bite the bullet and suppress their pain.

The way a wolf takes down a deer underscores the primal need a man has to protect his gut. The wolf goes either for the deer's throat or the stomach, the two most vulnerable spots. Similarly, a human male's instinctive response to thousands of years of fighting wars and withstanding dangerous situations is to tighten the solar plexus when the adrenal glands signal a threat, and to then clench the throat. While these are appropriate responses for the battlefield, they do not benefit men in interpersonal relationships.

When men begin inner work they often come up against the primal fear of vulnerability. They may encounter lifelong patterns of holding tension in their bellies, chests, and shoulders, and such patterns are not easy to undo. Increased sensitivity may initially take the form of greater irritability. Some men, particularly those who suppress a lot of anger, find their emotional fuses considerably shorter. They may feel touchy at first, simply because they are not yet comfortable being seen with their guard down. And the transformation process is certainly not made easier by the fact that employers and colleagues are generally not sympathetic to one's newly discovered feelings of sensitivity and vulnerability.

With time, however, the sense of vulnerability gives way to greater emotional receptivity and availability. Men discover a wider and deeper emotional base from which to express themselves in relationships. Although the process of change might be rough going for a while, their partners usually find them much more alive, responsive and present as the walls come down. Regardless of gender, a partner's ability to be present for the other person is always equal to how present he or she is with themselves. Heavy emotions like anger and rage, once opened into with awareness, reveal a softness and vulnerability at their core. Grief, when it is embraced, eventually opens us to compassion. Fear, once accepted, softens into love. Certainly not all feelings need to be expressed, but they do need to be honored.

While for centuries women were taught to please men rather than listen and respond to their own inner truths, the feminist movement has helped turn the tide in the West and elsewhere. Despite enormous advances, however, many women still carry a deep sense of unworthiness in their hearts and minds. Centuries of male domination have inculcated into many women such core beliefs as: *I am not good enough, My voice does not count, I need to please a man to be fulfilled.* The primal pain of this conditioning can't help but have an affect on a woman's self-worth and empowerment, sexual pleasure and self-confidence. Some women continue to turn to men to express their own inner power. Others learn to "act like males" and wind up feeling less than authentically themselves. Still others—choosing a healing path—open again to their inner feelings, reclaiming their intuitive wisdom and voices in the process. But the journey is not without its share of pain.

Women who choose to open their hearts again often find tremendous pain below the surface. Suppressed anger, sadness, fear, and rage often come into awareness as they consciously turn within for healing. Emotional healing for women and men is somewhat like flushing clean water through a dirty hose. At first the water is cloudy, but eventually, as the hose is purified, the water becomes clear. Similarly, as women release their pain and deepen their own centers through self-reflection, meditation, and other forms of healing work, discomforts can arise, and communication can be rough. But clarity will follow, and they will eventually find a deeper, clearer center from which to interact with the world.

Women who make the inner healing journey—accessing their spiritual core—discover that their wholeness is not dependent upon men. This inner sense of wholeness becomes the basis of a deeply nurturing, spiritual partnership. They discover a renewed ability to give without being depleted and without fostering dependency in their loved ones. Women discover the joy of receiving love, as they no longer live in fear of male power and domination. They also learn to trust their instincts, refusing to give away their minds and bodies to needy, unwholesome males for love, appreciation, and approval.

Women have much to teach men about emotional depth and living from the heart. The rational mind has a vital place in life, but it must be quieted for us to experience real intimacy. Our minds are trained to analyze data, but it takes the heart and feeling to truly appreciate a flower, a child, a man or a woman in their wholeness. The heart understands the higher mathematics of synergy in which the whole is greater than the sum of its parts. But it doesn't have to think about it, or analyze it.

Over the last three decades there has been an emphasis on the more feminine attribute of feeling in Western psychology, and this can be seen as a reaction to a long standing overemphasis on the more masculine attribute of intellect. Many of us believe that the devaluing of feeling is a basic cause of interpersonal violence and cultural and ecological destruction. It's doubtful there can ever be any substantial peace in the world until women, the custodians of the feeling mode, are fully emancipated and in positions of authority. On a smaller scale, the same holds true in our own homes.

No individual who is truly in touch with his feelings would intentionally harm women, children, or men, let alone wipe out rainforests, or strip-mine mountains and valleys to satisfy a need for profit. As the heart opens, we discover a deep kinship with life, an ability to share other points of view and to think, speak, and listen with greater clarity and comprehension. Being in touch with our feelings brings us into alignment with the larger community of which we are a part.

A whole person is balanced in head and heart. With a quiet mind and an unguarded heart he or she can embrace the chaos of existence without the need to judge, dominate, or change it.

KISSED BY THE BELOVED: FAMILY PATTERNS OF FEELING

Every summer and fall for years, my (David's) father would go off to the mountains or deserts of the Northwest, where he could be found sitting on the black granite rock watching Chinook salmon swimming up the whitewater flow of the Imnaha River in the Wallowa Mountains, or hunched up under sagebrush near a water hole, waiting for antelope down in the Jordan Valley of Southeast Oregon. For ten of those years, I (David) was like a shadow by his side absorbing his understanding like moss does rain. In a way, my father became my first teacher in sitting meditation. Somehow, out there in the wilds with my father, I began to contemplate the mystery of it all. I was kissed by the Beloved in the form of Mother Nature.

Less than a hundred years ago American Indians were living throughout the country where we live in Oregon. Their native tongues still speak to us in the names of rivers and mountains: David's favorite summer swimming hole up at the headwaters of the Tualatin; the Necanicum, where fisherman still pull out ten pound steelhead; the Nehalem, where David trout fished every summer as a kid; and to the east the icy turquoise waters of the Metolius winding its way through tall forests of Ponderosa Pine. The names are a fading reflection of a native culture that left not one scar on the earth. They walked a path with heart and stayed close to the feeling of the Mother.

What are the messages you received as a child about the importance of feelings? As part of our journey to spiritual partnership and the Beloved, it's important to investigate such early programming.

Below is a list of questions to help you understand how your feelings have been programmed by family patterns.

- Did your parents honor their own feelings? Did they honor yours?

- Was it safe to express your emotions, no matter how intense or varied?

- Was it encouraged in your home to talk about your feelings?

- Did you witness your parents openly expressing themselves, whether sad or angry?

- Did you ever feel like you wanted to cry, but couldn't?
- Did you ever feel like you wanted to scream, but couldn't?
- Did you ever get the feeling in your body that something was being kept from you?
- Were you ever given the message that as a girl you were too sensitive?
- Were you ever given the message that as a boy you were too sensitive?
- Did you ever get the message that feeling was inferior to reason?
- Did your family ever make biased jokes or comments against women? Sensitive males?

We often uncover our core beliefs in moments of emotional agitation. Anytime we locate a core belief, the key is to make contact with the feeling behind it. As we bring our awareness to the feeling, it will gradually begin to dissolve. It can sometimes take years, for deeply ingrained thought patterns to be completely eliminated. But as we become more aware of the core beliefs we've held onto since childhood, the damage they cause can be greatly minimized.

Try speaking the following core beliefs aloud, and see if there is any reaction (like tension) in your body.

- It is not safe to cry.
- I shouldn't feel this way.

- It's wrong to show anger.
- Fear is a sign of weakness.
- Loving couples don't yell.
- This pain is going to kill me.
- God punishes us for our pleasure.
- Feeling is inferior to reason.
- Chaos is not safe.
- It is not safe to speak my truth.
- I am too sensitive.

Ultimately, our feelings are no more real than the myriad thoughts that flicker in our minds. If we learn to listen to what we're feeling, though, we are led inward toward greater clarity and intuitive understanding. Then, like invisible tentacles flowing out into the atmosphere, our feelings put us in touch with life around us. Such awareness is an essential component of kindness, strength, wisdom, intelligence, and relationship.

SEXUAL CONDITIONING

There is no energy more fundamental to life than sexual energy. It is the primal force of life, responsible for virtually every stage of maturation from conception to death. Therefore, the sexual conditioning we receive from our families and our culture goes straight to the core of our identity. It literally hits us right in the heart. Our deepest issues reside below the belt, but they are healed in the heart.

The most powerful effect of negative sexual conditioning is that it causes an apparent separation between the heart and the genitals. It happens when our sexuality is paired with guilt, shame, and fear, and the conscious mind is thus forced to reject the most primal, intimate part of our nature. The caring heart is, in effect, forced to dissociate from its root nature.

Poor self-esteem, chronic physical and emotional tension, depression, general hostility, and fear of intimacy are common symptoms of sexual repression. Once our sexual energy is divorced from the healing heart, the sexual act is no longer perceived or experienced as an opportunity for true intimacy and lovemaking. Rather, it simply becomes a way to release tension. It becomes a vehicle for temporarily eliminating the inner stress caused by our repression. This tends to intensify feelings of separateness (thus strengthening the ego) and generate suffering as our partners become mere objects of self-gratification.

Many of us experienced the separation of sexual energy and heart in our adolescence. Fucking, as distinct from lovemaking, was often the main focus of attraction between the sexes, and women were sometimes regarded as "pieces of meat." Care for the heart was often painfully absent. The modern day bar scene and the focus on the body in all forms of advertising also epitomize the same phenomenon. Sadly, much of our culture and many of our families teach us to separate the heart from our genitals by forcing our sexuality into the basement of the unconscious, away from feelings, away from concepts of God, Nature, health, and intimacy. Any form of sexual violation deepens and solidifies the wound, fostering yet a greater sense of distrust and basic alienation.

It is precisely this separation between the heart and sexual center that is at the core of sexual abuse. Sexual abuse can only arise in an individual who feels utterly divided within himself. It can only manifest when the heart is cut off from the sexual center, when sexual energy, perceived as separate from the whole, is repressed. Such fragmentation magnifies one's sense of duality, increasing inner tensions and finally giving rise to the compulsive need for release.

The experience of true intimacy requires a healthy, wholesome, attitude toward our sexuality. We simply cannot separate our hearts from our sexual energy and feel truly connected. Love requires that we surrender, yet how can we do so when our bodies and minds hold the painful associations of guilt, shame, or sexual abuse? In order to feel truly intimate with our partners, we need to examine our sexual conditioning.

In traditional societies like the American Indian nations, the onset of puberty was ushered in by a rite of passage honoring the progression from the unconsciousness of childhood to the awareness of adulthood. In such cultures, this stage in a young person's life was also recognized as a time of intensified spiritual and psycho-sexual powers. Unlike in Western society, where women have been thought "unclean" during their menstrual flow, girls were honored when they began to menstruate. It was a sign of emerging power and a deepening of their primal connection to nature. Needless to say, there was no such thing as PMS in such cultures.

Young men were likewise respected and carefully guided into the proper use of their new found sexual energies. No guilt. No shame. No embarrassment. Such healthy attitudes toward their sexuality helped them engage in the dance of relationship with deep respect and honor for their feminine counterparts.

In old cultures like India, Tibet, and China, there is still an understanding in some communities that lovemaking is nothing less than communing with God. It is a reenactment of the wedding of the Masculine/Feminine forces (Shiva-Shakti) from which life as we know it has emerged. Through Taoist and Tantric sexual practices sexual energy is transmuted into a spiritual celebration of unity, with immense healing capacities for our whole being, including our relationships.

Many spiritual seekers are confused about the connection between the drive for enlightenment and the desire for sexual expression. Such confusion is primarily the manifestation of unconscious conditioning. Sexual energy is perceived as impure, tainted, and unholy. Again, we would argue that such conflict derives from negative programming resulting in the apparent separation between the heart and the genitals. Such separation results in a deep seated fear of intimacy. The spiritual quest, often with an emphasis on purity and conservation of sexual energies, becomes an acceptable way to avoid real intimacy and the often painful conditioning held around it. One need only look to the clergy and the various scandals associated with covert sexual behavior to recognize the often horrifying repercussions.

Sexual energy is integral to virtually every phase of physical and psycho-spiritual growth. It is the sap that gets transformed into all the various branches and flowers of human manifestation. It is the energy that drives the formation of our physical bodies when we are young. It is the healing energy that nurtures us back to wholeness when we are ill. It is the creative energy that fosters personal expression, innovation, and problem solving. It is the primal creative energy of God that opens the doors of spiritual perception, aiding us in our spiritual quest and the final dissolution of our egos. Sexual energy is the basis of the evolution of all life everywhere. To repress it is to deny immense creative intelligence. In a spiritual partnership sexual expression becomes a doorway into the heart and a pathway to healing. At this point, it would be helpful for us to again consider the programming we might have received from our family or from the culture at large.

The following questions are designed to help us investigate our sexual programming.

- What messages about sex did you receive from your family and culture?
- Do you recall receiving the message that sex was nasty or something to be ashamed about?
- Were you informed that masturbation was bad?
- Did your parents joke about sex, or approach the subject in a derogatory way?
- Did your parents establish appropriate boundaries concerning nudity? Can you describe these boundaries?
- Were you ever inappropriately touched by a family member, or friend? Did you discuss this with your parents? If so, how were you received?
- Were you ever informed of the sacred –spiritual—nature of sexual energy?
- Did you undergo any kind of special acknowledgment as you matured into womanhood or manhood?
- What was the emotional experience like the first time you had intercourse? Was it a nurturing experience?
- Have you ever made love to someone to gain approval, love, or appreciation? How did you feel afterward?

Did you receive any of the following core beliefs about sexuality?

- Sex is wrong.
- My genitals are dirty.
- All men want is to have sex with me.
- It's not acceptable to say "no."
- If she loves me she will always have sex with me.
- I can't completely let go physically and emotionally during sex.
- God doesn't approve of hot sex.
- I don't trust men/women to be deeply present for me in a sexual and emotional way.

Sex in love is one of the most direct and powerful ways of nurturing the heart, especially at certain phases of relating. As we explore sex in a spiritual partnership, we will begin to become aware of any faulty programming that we might have acquired through negative past experiences. With refined and caring awareness, these patterns can be dissolved. Sometimes this process can feel quite delicate, like cutting away the bandages on a deep and painful wound. But since sexual wounding occurs in the context of a relationship, the healing will also happen in the context of relationship.

Following are additional categories of conditioning that are worth investigating in terms of their impact on your relationship as spiritual partners.

Your Relationship to
Your Opposite Sex Parent

We can gain a great deal of insight into our current relationship or marriage by investigating our relationship to our countergender or opposite sex parent. It is this parent who imprints most deeply in us the qualities we look for in a mate.

The inner feminine within a male is primarily shaped through his relationship to his mother, or a mother substitute. For example, a mother figure who has a strong fear of males might begin to distance herself from her son as he matures. Inwardly, in response to his mother, the son's inner portrait of the feminine will possibly grow to include (among other things) a theme of rejection. When the son matures and attempts to enter into an intimate relationship, there is a good chance that he will feel rejected by his partner. Whether his wife consciously wants it or not, she will tend to wear the projection of his inner feminine.

Likewise, the inner masculine inside each female is primarily shaped through her relationship to her father, or father substitute. A woman whose father was emotionally supportive and nurturing will carry these qualities as part of her inner masculine side. When she enters into an intimate relationship, she will tend to attract a nurturing, supportive male who will tend to fit the projection of her inner male.

However, there are other influences that go into the shaping of our inner opposites. Teachers, experiences with siblings and peers, cultural messages, potent events that imprint us either positively or negatively, all go to shape our inner lives. But our relationship to the countergender parent will still have the greatest impact on the shaping of our inner opposite and the choosing of a mate.

Here is an exercise to help clarify and heal the unique relationship we have with our opposite sex parent.

- Find a quiet space in which to do this exercise.
- Make a list of all the positive qualities associated with your opposite sex parent.
- Now make a list of all the negative qualities associated with this parent.
- Close your eyes, and see if you can locate these same qualities inside yourself. Find the feeling you associate with these qualities. On the positive side, does the particular quality bring up feelings of joy? Of pride? Of compassion? On the negative side, does it bring up feelings of fear? Anger? Sadness? Aversion?

As we open into such feelings we allow ourselves an opportunity to resolve the tensions still being held from past experiences. Such an exercise helps to break down the separation in the heart, allowing for forgiveness and healing. As we make peace with our parents we will discover a renewed sense of appreciation and care for our partners.

YOUR RELATIONSHIP TO YOUR SAME SEX PARENT

A boy's father unconsciously transmits to him everything he knows about being a man. This includes his relationship to money, God, sex, women, power and the world in general. As part of a man's healing, it is vital that he locate his father's consciousness within himself. He will draw on it for strength during times of difficulty. He will also discover that by introjecting (accepting without question) his father's consciousness, he has unwittingly absorbed his shadow of core beliefs and biases as well.

A girl's mother transmits to her daughter everything she knows about womanhood. This includes, among many other things, sex, God, nurturing, birthing children and caring for a family, creativity, power and navigating in the world. Any undigested past experiences involving betrayal, abandonment, physical abuse, and prejudice of any kind will also be unconsciously transmitted to her daughter. The daughter will carry her mother's history (both positive and negative) in the cells of her body and in her unconscious.

Again, let us do a healing exercise, this time centering on our same sex parent.

- Find a quiet place in which to do this exercise.
- Make a list of all the positive qualities you associate with your same sex parent.
- Now make a list of all the negative qualities you associate with this parent.
- Close your eyes and see if you can find any of these same qualities inside yourself. If you are a man, can you, for example, sense the connection between your father's distrust of women and your own? If you are a woman, can you, for example, sense the connection between your mother's unresolved anger toward men and your own?

As we welcome in the feelings associated with our parents, a healing happens. Awareness softens the tension we carry in our minds and bodies, and eventually we will find that we no longer need to act out such inherited patterns in our intimate relationships.

Concepts of God

Our concept of God has a profound impact on the way we relate to our partner, others in our life, and the world at large. Explore together your thoughts and feelings about God. Is He Male? If so, how might this impact your relationship to each other? Is She Female? If so, how might this impact your relationship? What if we have no concept for God?

Explore the messages you received in childhood regarding a Supreme Being. Did your parents or those associated with your religious or spiritual upbringing convey that this Being was loving? Fierce? Judgmental? All merciful? Such investigation of your respective spiritual conditioning has a profound influence on how the two of you navigate the territory of the shared heart and mind. Our intimate relationship subtly mirrors the dance we do with the Divine.

Other Areas of Childhood Conditioning

There are many other categories of conditioning worth exploring as spiritual partners—such as, money, power, loyalty/betrayal, and politics. Bringing our past conditioning into the light of day—into conscious awareness—is the first step toward changing or improving on it. We know from the teachings of psychology that we have to first become conscious of something before we can possibly change or improve it. When we look carefully at the patterns activated in our relationships, we are led back to earlier stages of growth when our nervous systems were softer, more impressionable, and thus more easily conditioned. Now, with greater awareness, we can make new choices. Since this process of acknowledging our past conditioning—and pain—can make us extremely vulnerable, it is important that we be kind to each other at this time. And that we realize we are blessed with a Master Healer within.

REMEMBER THE ONE!

The Beloved—the One Heart—is with us through every storm of forgetfulness, through every apparent loss or betrayal. It is the Beloved we first see reflected in the romance of our lover's face. It is the Beloved that empowers us with vitality and joy early on in our relationship. It is the Beloved in the form of a divine surgeon that strips us of our defenses and reveals our shadows. And it is the Beloved—the ground of pure being beyond the mind—that finally delivers us from the illusion of personal control, revealing the exquisite nature of the unguarded heart.

We are fundamentally loved, always have been, always will be. No circumstance or person can add to or take away from our intrinsic nature. It cannot be depleted nor improved upon. We are whole. As our lives move ever more in harmony with the Beloved we no longer seek approval or love in any external form from anything or anyone. From here our relationships become transparent, unencumbered, and free of demand. Finally, we come to the understanding that there simply is no other; just the Beloved at play, in drag, wearing billions of different costumes.

Once the spiritual eye opens we see that everything in our pasts, no matter how difficult and painful, fits into a greater plan. Nothing is ever out of place or out of time. Our lives, right down to the number of hairs on our head, as the Bible puts it, are exquisitely guided by the invisible hand of the Beloved. Sometimes life is very messy, but even when we are sitting right in the middle of the whole mess, we see that everything simply is. From the perspective of the Beloved there is no place for judgment. From the quiet space of the heart, compassion arises spontaneously. Our parents, grandparents, great grandparents, all the way back through time, played out the roles required of them by life. They were danced by the Dancer! Like all living beings, they wanted to be happy and avoid suffering. As hard as it is for the ego to accept when our dreams are shattered, things happen because they must. Given the vastness of the universe—and the unfathomable realm of cause and effect—we cannot expect to understand why.

CHAPTER FOUR

Faces in the Mirror

The world is no more than the Beloved's single face;
In the desire of the One to know its own beauty,
we exist. . . . Without reason, the clear glass
equally mirrors wisdom and madness.
—GHALIB

When we choose particular people as our partners, our psychological patterns tend to fit like a lock and key. However, this interlocking fit isn't always so obvious. For example, a man whose girlfriend has an unacknowledged fear of intimacy can find himself spontaneously wanting to pull back from her, without knowing that he is mirroring her unconscious pattern. Or a woman whose husband is judgmental of her volatile emotions may feel as if she's on an emotional roller-coaster in his presence, to the point of getting so irritated with him that she wants to scream. In fact, her unconscious is picking up on the chaotic emotions inside him, which he keeps in check but wants to set free. Or a man with a fear of abandonment will be attracted to a woman with a pattern of abandoning her partners. He feels like the victim until he begins to investigate his own shadow and his own unconscious pattern—and how well they fit with hers.

The shadow refers to all the different parts of us that we judge as bad, unacceptable, immoral, distasteful. Much of it originates in childhood. Facing our shadow can be upsetting at times, but in doing so we bring both depth and lightness to our hearts. Paradoxically, once we face our shadow, we realize we are not our shadow. When we know that we are not fundamentally our shadow, we no longer blame others for mirroring those dark aspects of ourselves. The shadow is a hindrance only when it goes unacknowledged.

WE ARE EACH OTHER'S SHADOW

We worked with a woman once, whom we'll call Penny, who was dealing with an alcoholic partner, whom we'll call Frank. As Frank was not ready to begin his healing, Penny came in for a session with Faye each week alone. Initially Penny had a great deal of anger and blame to discharge. The focus was almost entirely on the painful effects of Frank's unconscious, negative behavior. "He should change! If only he would stop drinking!" Over time, Penny began to soften as she realized that Frank was suffering at least as much as she was—and that her own behaviors were contributing to their distress.

As Penny began to focus on herself and to explore the roots of her own suffering, she turned inward—the first crucial step in healing. Gradually, Penny realized that she shared some common ground with Frank. They each had a frightened child inside. They each often denied their pain. And they both too often blamed the world and other people for their problems. But whereas Penny's conditioning led to a compulsion toward work, Frank's resulted in alcohol abuse. Penny and Frank were each reflecting suppressed facets of the other. What they couldn't face within themselves got projected outward.

> Every part of our personality that we do not love will become hostile to us.
> —ROBERT BLY, *A Little Book on the Shadow*

Such insight had profound, life-changing consequences in the way Penny began relating to her husband. She became receptive to an understanding of his pain. At odd moments, when her thoughts were stilled, she began to see a basic goodness flickering behind Frank's often clouded eyes. For brief moments, her thoughts didn't argue with what was, allowing her to feel compassion rise up spontaneously. His pain became hers. His predicament became hers as well. As Penny began to feel that the two of them were interconnected, not separate, the walls of her defenses started to crack, and the light of understanding streamed in.

At this point Penny was able to relinquish the judgments about Frank that she had held onto so fervently. Faye guided her in considering the core beliefs and feelings that had sustained her unhappy relationship with Frank. Penny realized that a fear of abandonment and guilt over early childhood events had set the stage internally for her partnership with him. Frank's verbally abusive nature was a fierce reflection of the thoughts and feelings she held inside herself but found difficult to confront. Penny's father had also been an alcoholic. And, like many children, Penny internalized her father's pain, feeling somehow responsible for his illness. She felt diminished, inadequate, and unworthy of being loved. Core beliefs like *I am worthless, I am bad,* and *I hurt the people I love,* solidified around Penny's emotional pain.

Working incessantly helped Penny keep her fears at bay. Work and achievement were her drugs of choice, allowing her to ward off the pain of her own unfinished past. Yet her feelings of inadequacy, guilt and fear persisted, often resulting in a low-grade depression and a growing inability to enjoy her many successes. Her life had reached the point where it was all she could do to muster up enough energy to climb the next mountain.

Frank provided a mirror of what Penny had been unable to come to terms with inside herself. His shortcomings represented her shadow side of unresolved pain, anger, and fear. In this sense, Frank was an important spiritual teacher for Penny, as his frailties—and her recognition of the same weaknesses within herself—became a potent catalyst for opening Penny's once guarded heart.

Frank and Penny finally decided to separate after many painful years. Yet what stood out to us was Penny's ability to separate without the intense blame that frequently accompanies such break-ups. She kept her heart open through the pain and agony of the actual divorce. Shortly after their separation, Penny called to acknowledge Frank for being the catalyst of such intense inner growth. The excruciating pain of their relationship—and her willingness finally to accept it without blaming either Frank or herself—was the pressure Penny needed to deal with the unhealed truths about herself and to open her heart in the process.

Recognizing that we often project our own shadow side onto our partner is a key to healing the heart. In owning our shadow side we experience that we are not separate from the one we sought to blame. We become receptive to the awareness of how we are interconnected. Ego, with the accompanying sense of separateness, is dissolved as we embrace this interconnectedness.

The turning point in Penny's healing came when she was finally able to whole-heartedly admit that the negative qualities she judged in Frank were aspects of her that until now she had been unable to examine. She no longer saw Frank as the bad guy but rather as someone struggling to overcome suffering, like everyone else. With this insight Penny shifted from a position of self-righteous intolerance to one of understanding and compassion. She felt Frank's pain as deeply as her own, ceased her argument with reality, and no longer blamed Frank for what could never be. Penny's opened heart allowed her to glimpse the freedom from judgment, that inner sky where no fences (defenses) separate us.

When we succeed in opening our hearts and knocking down our defenses, we come to understand that we are not our shadow nor are we the story that formed it. And neither are our partners. From such a diamond clear perspective, we can fully accept what is.

Acceptance of what is does not mean we avoid taking action when there is the need to change a bad situation. It is not a passive point of reference but a positive one. Acceptance comes from clearly seeing a situation for what it is, without judgment. This allows us to make decisions with greater awareness, compassion, and skill. The important decisions Penny finally made came not from a negative, fearful, mental reaction to her husband but rather from the quietness and clarity of her heart.

In his previously referenced work, *A Little Book on the Shadow*, Robert Bly talks about the aura of someone who has done their inner work:

When the shadow becomes absorbed the human being
loses much of his darkness and becomes light and playful
in a new way.

When we find ourselves reacting negatively to our partner's
behavior, we need to turn our attention inward and investigate
our own thoughts and feelings. We need to ask ourselves, what
might my partner's irritating behavior be reflecting about me?
What is the sensation arising in my chest when my partner raises
her voice? Why does my partner's love of money upset me? As
we investigate our own patterns more deeply, our knee-jerk reactions to our partner's behavior become less frequent. Such self-
inquiry serves to break down the duality between self and other,
and we experience a greater sense of interconnectedness.

Because of the mind's natural aversion to experiencing pain,
we all have a tendency to project our unwanted psychic material onto our partner. In other words, we make him or her
carry our painful shadow side. When our walls of defensiveness break down, however, destroying the social masks that
hide our shadow, we see ourselves and our partners more
clearly—and our intimacy deepens.

THE PROJECTION RULE OF THUMB

Since projecting our shadow side onto someone else is a defense mechanism, and a denial of reality, how can we know
when we are doing it? The Swiss psychiatrist Carl Jung used to
say that as a rule of thumb any time we react strongly to someone—whether that reaction is positive or negative—we are

probably projecting. That person becomes the target for those concepts and feelings that we find unacceptable in ourselves. Do specific behaviors cause our stomachs to tighten up? Do certain attitudes stimulate an emotional reaction inside? A little self-investigation will help us understand the meaning of such strong reactions. We discover that our reactions toward our partner tell us more about ourselves than about them. Owning our true thoughts and feelings becomes a crucial step in supporting the deeper well-being of our relationship.

Here is an example of projection. We find ourselves reacting strongly to our partner's critical nature. You shouldn't be critical, is the message we deliver. Our partner might indeed be critical, but the fact that we have an intense reaction to their behavior is indicative of our own unexamined critical nature. In other words, we judge in them the critical side of ourselves that we refuse to investigate.

What does projection tell us about conflict? Since the issue is not outside ourselves, healing the relationship begins with self-reflection and an investigation of our own hidden thoughts. For example, we might ask ourselves, what does my reaction to her judgmental nature tell me about myself? Why do I shy away from judging myself? What is the basis of my own judgmental nature? How does it feel to criticize myself? When we ask such questions of ourselves, the focus shifts from blame to healing, from the periphery of our awareness to the center.

Once we begin to understand the significance in our reactions—that, for example, being afraid of criticism is an indicator of our own inner critic, we can stop blaming each other, and the sense of separateness fades. The defensive me position shifts to we, and the feeling of love returns in a deeper, less guarded way.

HIDING FROM THE SHADOW

It is not uncommon as spiritual seekers to shun the descent into the shadow in favor of the high feelings associated with ascent. When we do so, however, we run the risk of empowering that which we try and avoid.

Spiritual growth is a coexistence of opposites. Sooner or later meditative practices energize our core patterns. To the extent that we try and side-step uncomfortable feelings that want to arise, we feed them. In this way, various negative tendencies stored in the subconscious can exert tremendous power over the spiritual seeker who tries to suppress them. One needn't look far in many of the contemporary spiritual organizations to see prime examples.

Pride, arrogance, hidden sexual compulsions, learned helplessness, and power-tripping are too often common features in such groups. The more we try to suppress the shadow, the stronger it grows. Add to this suppressive tendency the release of energy that comes from spiritual practices and the spiritual seeker can find himself in very rough waters. We can find ourselves moody, depressed, physically ill, angry, intolerant, sexually over-amped and anxious. The so-called cracked identity, our negative conditioning, has become magnified. In this regard, good psychotherapy can sometimes be useful for the western seeker in conjunction with his spiritual practices.

The danger in a spiritual partnership is that elevated concepts of charity, loving-kindness, generosity, and staying calm can be used to deny the heavier, darker aspects of our nature.

Eventually the energy generated by the yoga of our relationship—combined with spiritual practices—activates whatever is hidden. The more we try to suppress what wants to surface, the more potent it becomes. The following is a case in point.

Once during a counseling session with a couple who were into meditating, the topic of sex outside the marriage arose. Suddenly it felt very tense in the room. As we investigated the matter, it was revealed that the woman had an intense sexual/ emotional interest in another member of their spiritual group. The more she tried to suppress the attraction, the more powerful it grew. We suggested that they begin their investigation of their shadows by taking the taboo off the topic of having an extramarital relationship. Together we explored key questions. Is it natural to be attracted to other people? Is it bad? If so, why? What is the basis of this taboo? What are the possible consequences of having sex outside the marriage? What is at the heart of this attraction? Is it possible for us to love more than one person emotionally and sexually? What does the attraction have to teach us about the heart? Relationships? Love?

Such questions allowed the couple to open—relax —into the topic, rather than suppress it and become tense. It was, in part, the inability to face the taboo that fueled the attraction. As they opened into the issue, exploring thoughts that were previously labeled taboo, the attraction to the other person naturally diminished, and the intimacy between the couple was strengthened.

When we refuse to discuss certain key issues with our partner for fear that our dark side will be revealed, those issues take on greater significance. The more we try to control a shadow thought, the more it wants to have its way. On the other hand, when we're open about our fear, anger, sexual impulses or jealousy, we discover a middle way that is neither suppressive nor

overly expressive. The communication between us and our partner becomes clearer, and the positive energy between us expands.

Still, there's the question of how much we should share
with our partner. Must we share everything in an intimate
relationship? Although this is a very individual matter, a general rule is that anything which you feel can't be shared probably needs to be. When something we've done or pondered
causes our hearts to close, and this gets reflected in a distancing from our partner, it's good to share it. But this does not
mean that every questionable thought running through our
minds needs to be shared. As our attunement to one another
becomes more refined, we become more transparent anyway.
Our hearts will guide the way.

Given that we probably spend a lot of energy hiding from
it, how do we find our shadow? Reflecting on what we consider to be bad, inappropriate, or immoral will introduce us to
what lies hidden away out of fear. Or think of the things about
your partner that you strongly dislike. Your shadow lies in
those very things. Think of someone whose behavior you find
utterly disdainful. That behavior is your shadow.

If you want to engage in a powerful exercise, choose to do
consciously something you hold as a taboo. A whole ava-
lanche of suppressed thoughts and feelings will often surface,
many in defense of our established identity. Ordinarily the
conscious mind seeks to banish and control any thought, feeling, behavior, or person that threatens our self-image. Confronting that well-defended image by doing something that
you consider to be taboo will likely bring some astounding insights about yourself.

Confronting Your Shadow—
Healing Actions

Ask yourself: "What are the things I like least about my partner? What is it that irritates me—or makes me mad?"

- Now go even deeper inside yourself and find out if some of these traits are not your own. Get beneath your thoughts to the actual feelings. Does your partner's tone of voice ever remind you of a parent? An old lover? Yourself? Accept what you least like about your partner as a part of you that needs to be acknowledged.

- Notice your bodily reactions during arguments and think about why they're triggered. Most of the time conflict is a rehashing of old, unfinished business from the distant past that has not yet been fully acknowledged. Once we can truly and fully acknowledge it, face it squarely, we get free of it.

- Look into a mirror! The next time you find yourself verbally attacking your partner, literally pick up a mirror. Now repeat your remarks at him while looking at yourself. Who are we really angry at?

- The next time you find yourself reacting negatively to your partner, take a time-out. Go into a quiet room and feel the sensations in your body. Take this opportunity to own (contain) your projection, then evaluate what you need to communicate to your mate. When we are genuinely calmer, more centered, our communication will be more clear, and we will arrive at the truth more quickly.

- Question your assumptions. Next time you make a negative assumption about your partner, ask yourself: "Is this really true? Can I know this for certain?" Assume that your partner is sincere and honest when he or she communicates with you.

- Try on the concept that everything you see in the world is a projection of your mind. How does this change the way you perceive your partner?

- Remember that you are not your mind.

- In quiet meditation, reflect on a person you dislike. What does it feel like in your body to dislike someone? Where does this feeling of dislike reside? In the chest, perhaps? In the stomach?

Now visualize this individual you dislike standing in front of you. Look into his or eyes and try and find something good about them. See if you can connect with their essence. Now mentally send them love, affection, kindness. See them succeeding in life. See them achieving their goals. See them happy, calm, and healthy. Thank them for being a mirror for you.

When we make peace inside ourselves with an adversary out there, we are bridging aspects of ourselves. By closing the gap with this person, we are healing a separation between our own hearts and minds. We are welcoming home a forgotten and neglected part of ourselves. We often distance ourselves from others as a way of avoiding unresolved feelings inside us.

Jung once wrote that children often act out the unlived parts of their parents. We would add that our partners often act out the unlived parts of us.

WELCOMING THE SHADOW

In many traditional societies like Bali, Nepal, and India, the shadow archetypes are openly respected and honored. Throughout the year native people celebrate the various deities of the underworld. Whether in the form of the blood dripping Kali, Durga with Her mighty sword, or Lord Shiva with His love of cobras, the wrathful deities are welcomed into the community and symbolically praised, clothed and fed like real people. Mexico, Central and South America have similar rituals. The wisdom in this approach is manifest on different levels, but in essence it involves symbolically setting an extra place at the table for the dark faces of the Beloved. Such rituals teach us that by honoring—instead of trying to annihilate—the forces of the unconscious, their energies can be channeled into creative action. It's a symbolic way for the conscious and unconscious minds to welcome each other. Art also serves this function. The object of healing work is not to eliminate the shadow but to integrate it with the larger Self.

The archetype of the ancient Samurai can be useful to contemplate in this context: The Samurai was such a skilled warrior in part because he knew that the enemy did not really exist outside. The real battle was won or lost inside, between the various forces of heart and mind. It would be disastrous for the Samurai to try and eliminate his violent nature. Instead, the key was to bring awareness to it. This would allow him to channel his energy into appropriate creative action. Thus, the real skill for the Samurai was to remain anchored, open and alert within, pushing nothing away. When one is centered there is little chance of projection. Inwardly we remain calm, even detached. Outwardly we act with clarity, integrity and skill.

In our personal relationships we must challenge the tendencies of the mind to judge, blame, criticize, and refuse feedback. These are all indicators of ego. One simple question will begin to unravel our deception: *What thoughts and feelings am I avoiding now?* In this way attention will get turned inward toward its source, we will become receptive to insight and understanding, and conflict will be healed at its root. If we face ourselves in this way, acknowledging that we are mirrors for each other, our relationship will remain fresh and alive.

The most important thing is staying present for whatever wants to arise. Our presence—awareness—is the gifted healer in any situation. Daily spiritual practices like prayer and meditation are enormously helpful in this regard.

MERCY

It seems that we cannot grow without some shadow. As long as the journey continues there will be some resistance to our footsteps. Wholeness, we discover, is a coexistence of opposites, not the annihilation of one in favor of another. We have to make room for opposing views. There will always be some mysterious part of us that remains a little out of reach. Absorbing the shadow does not eradicate the darkness. But the poison of our shadow can become medicine. It is a process of integration, not annihilation. In love, we learn to live with all of our selves.

When we look into our partner, we see into ourselves. Stripped down to the heart, we are not different. We long for love. We shy away from pain. Heartache can become heartsong as we relax into the experience of the moment, whatever it might be. Shadow-work is pure mercy. It humbles us. It holds the hands of a stranger. It takes the thorn out of the closed heart.

Up to this point we've shared a great deal about psychological patterns and how they get acted out between us. Now, before we enter Part Two, we want to put into a nutshell exactly how our patterns and core beliefs develop, how they are maintained, and what you can do to dismantle them. We will introduce the use of affirmations and mantras as skillful methods to dislodge the deep-rooted reactive patterns in the mind.

CHAPTER FIVE

Dismantling Negative Patterns

If you don't subject wheat to the grinding
millstone how will bread ever come
to decorate your table?
—RUMI

As a red-haired, spunky, young girl, Martha received disciplinary spankings from her father periodically throughout her childhood. As an adult, Martha found herself caught in a destructive pattern of being attracted to and having relationships with physically abusive males. As Martha reflects on the situation today, she becomes aware of a thought pattern she carries within herself: *It hurts to love a man.* Her ingrained belief cuts to the heart of the matter, but it wasn't until she was able to investigate her past and carefully examine her inner dialogue that she began to associate her attraction to violent men with her experiences of being physically assaulted by her father.

As a sensitive ten-year-old boy, Todd was emotionally overwhelmed by his parents' divorce. As an adult he has great difficulty committing to a long-term relationship; he becomes anxious and confused when approaching the point of real emotional intimacy with a partner. After bringing his focused attention to the thought patterns he's been living with for years, Todd now hears clearly the inner message he's been communicating to himself: *Love means loss.* It's a simple core belief but one that is loaded with emotional content. Todd's avoidance of committed relationships is an unconscious attempt to avoid reviving the pain associated with his parents' divorce.

Core beliefs, based on potent past experiences, become the unconscious window frames through which we attempt to interpret and organize the various events in our life. These beliefs define the individual ego, with its set patterns of thought and emotional reactivity. Left unchallenged, core beliefs can confine us and our relationships to limited, unwholesome, habituated modes of thought, feeling, and behavior.

Emotional defenses like denial, avoidance, and displaced anger crystallize around our core beliefs. They serve as protective shields against the pain associated with early childhood experiences. Each time a life event resonates sufficiently with the earlier seed impression, our emotional defenses mechanically kick into action, along with the corresponding core belief, forming an unconscious reactive pattern that attempts to distance us from both the present perceived threat and the primary negative experience. The deeper the wound, the more intense the defensive reaction. When some seemingly random event in our relationship triggers a faint memory of the earlier experience, we can suddenly find ourselves in a habituated pattern of blame and denial that prevents us from acknowledging and feeling the original pain. Often this involves distancing ourselves from our partner. But the root of the problem does not reside in our partner. It is in the internal unresolved pain of our past.

THE FOUR STAGES OF HEALING RELATIONSHIP CONFLICT

So how do we dismantle the negative (reactive) patterns that prevent us from enjoying a spiritual relationship with our partner, ourselves and the Beloved? In the first example above, Martha needs to reflect on her own core beliefs and feelings, the ones that support a pattern of abusive relationships, rather than blame her male partners. She has to turn within as a first step toward cultivating a stable, nurturing relationship. In the second example, for Todd to cultivate a committed relationship he also has to listen to the underlying thought patterns (core beliefs) and feelings of fear that cause him to avoid intimacy with loved ones. He too must turn within for the answer. But turning within is just the first step in dismantling negative patterns and resolving conflicts in our relationships.

There are essentially four stages to healing conflict in a relationship.

1. **Turning Within:** Owning our projections of anger, fear, and other emotional responses, and reflecting on underlying thought patterns.

2. **Becoming Receptive:** Opening to the full experience, including our partner's pain and point of view.

3. **Recognizing Our Interdependence:** Realizing the essential truth that we are not separate at the level of the heart.

4. **Resting in the heart:** Transcending the mind (our conditioning) so that we are no longer identified with our stories but are at peace both internally and with our partner.

Let's explore each of these healing stages and discover how they can help us to achieve greater peace with our partners and a deeper union with the Beloved.

Turning Within

We begin the healing process by bringing our attention to our inner landscape. By turning within, rather than battling it out with our partners, we reverse the outward flow of attention. As we take the focus (and blame) off our partner, we must assume that our partner is well meaning and not the true cause of our distress. This is not always so easy, given how we're used to thinking about problems between us. But shifting our focus like this allows us not only to connect with our own experience but to see our partner in a clearer light.

For example, when we feel irritated with our partner, we can bring our full awareness to that sense of irritation and avoid blaming them. When we feel afraid, we embrace the fear rather than displacing it onto our partner. When we feel angry, we own it and resist the tendency to tag it to our partner's behavior. If we listen carefully to our irritation, fear or anger, what usually surfaces is one of our core beliefs. For example: I'm afraid I'll be judged for sharing what I really feel. Or, Nothing I do is ever good enough. Or, My loved ones always leave me. As we open to this process of self-investigation, it soon becomes evident that most of our negative reactions to our partner are rooted in the past.

In establishing contact with each thought and feeling as it arises, our tendency to react out of anger or fear diminishes. In this way our attention gradually cuts through our reactive pattern, and we no longer find ourselves caught in the habitual push-button modes of behavior. The key is to turn our attention completely around–inward rather than outward—so that we face ourselves squarely.

Becoming Receptive

When we stop projecting the cause of our distress onto our partner, when we give up the blame game, we allow ourselves to become receptive to the emotional truth about ourselves. Turning within does not mean turning away from our partner and his or her experience; it means taking the focus—and the blame—off the other person so that we can face ourselves and the true cause of our unease. When we cease such projecting onto our partner, we spontaneously begin to open to the entire experience of what is. Our awareness expands. We become willing to touch the pain in our partner as well as in ourselves. Absolutely nothing gets pushed away. Once we actually connect with the raw, naked quality of a particular feeling, no matter how painful, we experience a letting go.

Becoming receptive is a crucial step because we come to realize that there is no difference between our pain and that of our partner; there is just pain. This acknowledgment helps mend our sense of separateness. When we turn within and open ourselves up to the truth, the unwholesome gap between self and other is bridged. When we move beyond concept and open fully to the pain of the moment, we find ourselves receptive and able to listen. Now we can reflect. Now we can share with each other from a clear inner space, taking into account our partner's point of view as well as our own. As we open ourselves in this way, we realize that there are no strangers in the heart.

In virtually any disagreement the shifting of attention off the other as a source of blame is a pivotal moment; it marks the moment of self-referral and the first step in the dismantling of our reactive patterns. Turning within and becoming receptive to whatever feelings arise within and between us is a master key to healing. Paradoxically, once we are able to listen internally, hearing our partner becomes effortless. Often during a conflict, we want to be heard—without first carefully listening to our partner. This is simply a defense mechanism to avoid our pain. Our words will not be clear and will not have the desired result if we are not able to open both inwardly to our self and outwardly to our partner, taking his concerns equally to heart. To become open and unmasked in this way requires in us a willingness to feel whatever amount of pain is present in the moment.

Recognizing Our Interdependence

Once we make contact with the root of our unease, free from the projected fantasies of the mind, it soon becomes clear that we are not rigid, separate entities—like wooden characters on a chessboard—but truly connected and interdependent beings. We are dancing partners. Your needs and my needs now become our needs. Your pain and my pain now becomes our pain. Doubts and suspicions generated by our split minds dissolve and get replaced with a heartfelt sense of cooperation. A whole new level of potential energy awakens between us as we transcend the rut of our emotional reactivity and realize that it only serves to reinforce our separateness. Finding solutions to our differences becomes relatively easy once we recognize how interdependent we are. But this fresh understanding does not typically arise all at once or without struggle.

Feelings of profound vulnerability can awaken with the acknowledgment of our shared needs. Waves of fear can arise, which are rooted in early childhood experiences of betrayal and abandonment. Because the ego does not want to recognize our interdependence, and because its survival depends on the illusion of being autonomous and separate, we may find ourselves striving to maintain our distance in an attempt to avoid being hurt. The realization of our interdependence is usually a gradual awakening. In this period when we're learning about our interdependence even as our ego is rebelling, a new level of understanding emerges, and a deep kindness and caring is felt in our relationship. Eventually, the recognition of our interdependence will extend beyond the borders of our relationship to include our larger family, our community, and the world. Such is the fruit of a marriage dedicated to acceptance and wholeness.

Resting in the Heart

Finally we must come to the understanding that we are not the mind. In cutting through our identification with the mind, all forms of spiritual practice can be helpful.

The various dramas we find ourselves caught up in are accompanied by a particular story, each of which is tied to the machinations of the mind. And yet even minimal self-reflection reveals that we exist prior to the mind. There is an awareness that is greater than the mind, that contains the mind. It is this awareness that gets cultivated through spiritual practice.

As we bring attention to our spiritual partnership it becomes evident that there is a place inside us that remains untouched by the dramas generated by our minds. When we are in this place, we call it simply resting in the heart. In letting go of our identification with the mind—and all its judgments, defenses, and false assumptions—we become quiet and peaceful. We find rest. It is while we are resting in the heart that we can see our reactive patterns for what they are—and finally dismantle them. It happens automatically. When we are resting in the heart, we understand that we are not our patterns of behavior or our minds or our relationship. We are part of the Beloved, and our home is in the Silence.

CONSCIOUS COMMUNICATION

Each stage of conflict resolution is a refinement in communication. We begin by coming into contact with ourselves, by turning within. We attune to the language of thought and feeling. Perhaps we are feeling frightened and we notice a pounding in our chests. Or we feel attacked and notice a tightening in our bellies, and have the thought to run. Or we feel lonely and have the thought that nobody understands us. Each thought and feeling is a form of self-communication. Once we are able to connect to our experience internally—and it can happen in a heartbeat—we spontaneously become open to the total situation. Now, whatever might be present between ourselves and our partner, pleasant or unpleasant, is open for investigation. From the heart we realize that the essential purpose of communication is to unify.

When we can communicate by staying centered in our own experience, rather than interpreting our partner's experience for them, we facilitate healing. When we can use our own feelings as the reference point, rather than blaming our partner, we know we're on the right track. For example, we can make such self-reflective, non-blaming statements as: "When you failed to come home for dinner three nights last week, I got scared—and that's why I reacted." Or, "When you get mad at me, I am afraid that you'll leave me." Staying focused on our own feelings is the conscious way to communicate with our partner. Blame and accusation are defensive reactions that do not get to the root of our feelings, which is why our use of them never resolves a conflict.

Conscious communication also involves paying close attention to the words we use when we speak with our partner. Does accusing our partner of being an unthoughtful idiot encourage healing? Or does it perpetuate his thoughtless behavior? Does calling a loved one an ass when he abruptly leaves a discussion bring clarity to the situation? Or does it foster illwill and blame? Labels deny our wholeness—and constrict the heart. When what we want is positive change in our relationship it is more effective to communicate with words that accurately describe how our partner's attitude or behavior feels to us. For example, "When you walk out of the room in the middle of a discussion, I feel dismissed. Is this your intent?" This kind of language grounds us. It pinpoints our relationship in present time from our perspective. It allows for investigation. It also gives our partner a positive opportunity to reflect on his behavior, which is essential for conflict resolution. The question at the end allows for clarity to flow between us and helps us to avoid making wrong assumptions. Our partner has space to respond. Using language that is nonviolent and allowing for change creates a bridge to connect us at a deeper level in a way that incorporates both our experiences. On the other hand, simply calling our partner an ass will tend to immediately raise the drawbridge between us; he will probably feel attacked and get defensive. The effect of name-calling is to separate, not unify, and it therefore defeats the purpose of communication.

When we focus on the other as the cause of our internal state, we lose touch with what's happening internally, and the tension and distance between us is reinforced. By communicating to our partner what our own experience is, in the moment, we eventually integrate the unconscious energy associated with our reactive patterns, and thus bring a deeper presence into the relationship. Then, if we need to ask for something from our partner, we can do so without any guilt or blame attached. For example, "Please don't walk away in the middle of an important conversation." Or "I need you to call me when you're going to be late." We can express ourselves as firmly—even as fiercely—as we need to if we do so from our heart center, without blaming the other person. In this way, our words will lack the hostility and judgment that arise in conjunction with a reactive pattern.

Here is an example of communicating wisely to resolve conflict.

Mary and Doug had spent an intimate weekend together at the coast. During this time, they made love, they cooked for each other, they took long walks on the beach and shared their hearts. By Tuesday of the following week, however, Mary was aware that the feeling of emotional warmth she and Doug had experienced on the weekend had given way to a cool distance.

Over the next few days she reflected on her feelings and what was going on inside her. By Thursday she asked Doug if they could spend the evening together and share their hearts. Mary began by sharing her observation of a growing distance between them. She talked about how, when this happens, they don't communicate as well or accomplish simple things around the home together with as much ease and joy. Being a musician, Mary compared her experience to one of playing a duet out of tune.

As Mary continued sharing with Doug, she became aware that she had felt shy and hesitant to speak about her feelings earlier in the week because she was afraid it would cause conflict and that Doug might think she was asking for too much. Her fear of conflict had caused her to doubt her intuition and to hold back initially.

Doug appreciated Mary's forthrightness and honesty. Her openness had created a sense of safety in him so that he was also

able to share. He volunteered that when he feels a distance between them, it touches on a fear of abandonment, which causes
him to drift off into his own world for protection rather than
reach out and initiate contact. And in this way, the distance between them grows even greater. Doug assured Mary that the
need for sharing time was never too much to ask of him. In fact,
he appreciated the opportunity to strengthen their intimacy.

In Mary's and Doug's conversation, there was no blame, accusation, or calling of names. Each spoke from their own centers. And the result? Their hearts opened once again—yet even
deeper—and the tension between them dissolved. The purpose of communication—to unify—hit its mark.

The alchemy of couples communicating honestly and without blame is that the separation between them is bridged. The
desire of the heart to restore unity guides the communication—and the instruments are retuned. Although the unifying
nature of love often becomes a catalyst for turning away from
love by bringing up unconscious separation, open and nonviolent communication is the way to navigate back into unity.

Here is another example of the skillful art of communication.

Leslie and Paul were enjoying a renewal in their marriage as
they celebrated their tenth anniversary. Leslie had recently en-
rolled at an art school to fulfill a life-long dream of painting,
but as a result a number of changes were brought about in
their marriage. Schedules, employment, finances, mutual sharing time, and household roles were all undergoing a substantial reorientation. With tensions mounting, Leslie and Paul
finally created time to share.

Paul started the conversation by saying that he was feeling afraid and insecure about Leslie's new direction. He was unsure about his place in Leslie's heart and feared she would meet someone new with the same artistic interest. Paul was also experiencing intense feelings of jealousy and possessiveness, even though he respected Leslie's courage for taking on a new challenge. Sharing his feelings in this way also made Paul feel vulnerable. First of all, he had never felt such an intense knot in his heart before. It literally felt like he had a fist in his chest. Secondly, he had never considered himself a jealous or possessive person, and he knew that jealousy and possessiveness were not love, yet this was his experience. So he was worried about how Leslie would respond to him in such a messy emotional state.

Leslie's heart was deeply touched by Paul's vulnerability and honesty. She honored his courage to share himself so deeply. Then Leslie shared about her experience of the first two weeks in her new undertaking. It had taken Leslie several years after her first inner prompting to feel confident enough to attend art school. Her insecurity about her creative abilities was huge. Leslie's first days at school were filled with a ray of joy pulsating through her for simply saying "yes" to her longing. At other moments, the critic inside would kick in and have a heyday with thoughts like, "Who do you think you are?" And, "You'll never amount to anything as a painter! Look at how much better these other students are . . ." Thoughts of being selfish also arose, as well as feelings of guilt for making decisions that brought her so much joy. But she found the strength to go forward anyway, and the negative thoughts eventually subsided.

Leslie shared with Paul her appreciation for his support over all the years. They shared a deep bonding that had been cultivated through many powerful life experiences. It was, in part, the strength of their relationship that gave Leslie the confidence to embark on her new journey, and she was grateful for that.

Paul's heart was soothed as he opened to Leslie's experience. Through their communication he relaxed into the opportunity to trust in their love and to breathe through his fears and insecurities as they arose. He came to realize that this vulnerable territory of the heart was his own new curriculum. Leslie's acceptance of him without judgment was a gift that supported him to open further.

Over the next two years of Leslie's art school education, Leslie and Paul committed to sharing deeply about the challenges they would confront as the flower inside each one's heart continued opening, petal by petal. The fact that Leslie and Paul could share from their hearts, without blame, accusation, or threat, allowed them to encounter life's changes in a way that would nurture and transform them both.

USING AFFIRMATIONS TO DISLODGE NEGATIVE CORE BELIEFS

Once we identify our negative core beliefs by observing the relationship patterns we habitually fall into, what can we do to dislodge those beliefs? Let's say that we have identified the core belief, *If I get too close to someone, they'll abandon me,* as the one that makes us afraid of intimacy. Or, *I don't deserve a kind person as a mate because I'm essentially inadequate,* as the core belief that makes us attracted to critical partners. Each relationship pattern is connected to specific, individual core beliefs. By paying attention to thoughts that arise during a confrontation with our partner, thoughts that are particularly conclusive and generalized, we can home in on the core beliefs that underlie our reactions.

But how do we begin to eradicate such beliefs? Affirmations can help. When we uncover a core belief, we can craft an affirmation to help uproot it and reframe our thinking. Affirmations are not magic bullets. Alone, they are not enough to completely dislodge unconscious negative thought patterns. However, they can help to undermine the ego's false sense of control. Used wisely, affirmations can be effective reminders of the deeper reality beyond our conditioning. Following is a list of common core beliefs, with the corresponding affirmations that can help eradicate them. Feel free to use these affirmations in anyway you like. You might want to keep a notebook and write down one or two affirmations every day for a month or more. Or make a tape recording of appropriate affirmations and listen to it while driving in the car, or in the morning when you first awake. Make up your own affirmations and consider them as spiritual pointers. An affirmation should ring true in your heart. Whether an affirmation works or not is up to God.

Affirmations work to the extent that they resonate with the deeper truth of our being. We have to bring a full, open awareness to our thoughts and feelings for affirmations to really be effective. Notice the erroneous thinking that so often runs through your mind—the judgments, comparisons, gossip, and condescension toward your self and others. All such negative thoughts arise from a lack of connectedness to the Beloved. Affirmations can help us to forge that connection.

CORE BELIEF	AFFIRMATION
I can never get enough love.	My heart is the source of infinite love.
Men/women abandon me.	Intimacy is safe. God never abandons me.
I can never do enough.	I love myself for who I am, not what I do. God does everything.
My aliveness causes other people pain.	My aliveness is a gift from God.
If I speak the truth I am afraid he/she will leave me.	I can speak the truth and never abandon myself.
I have to be in a relationship	The Beloved is all I need to be happy.
Men love me for my body.	Men secretly love me because I love God first.
I am responsible for my partner's happiness.	I am responsible for my own happiness. God is the source of everyone's happiness.
To need somebody is a sign of weakness.	To need somebody is beautiful. It reminds me of my need for the Beloved.

A word of warning about affirmations: Don't use them to try and suppress uncomfortable feelings that want to arise. Accept whatever comes up. Do, however, use affirmations like a gardener who sprinkles seeds onto fertile soil, carefully watering and nurturing them with love and attention, but then trusting that the seeds will grow. Plant your affirmations and then let them go. At the same time, cultivate the stillness of being—the source of all manifestation—through meditation. Act on what you know to be true and relax as much as possible when a negative thought pattern surfaces. An affirmation is a powerful thought that affirms a deeper truth. While some negative patterns may never change, affirmations can greatly minimize the damage such patterns can do.

MANTRA AND MEDITATION

A timeless means of dislodging negative thought patterns is the use of special mantras. Mantras are spiritually empowered sounds handed down through many generations of sages, which, when used properly, serve to purify the subconscious of negative thought patterns.

The true scientists of consciousness—sages and shamans around the world—realized long ago the limited effectiveness of analyzing thought as a way of getting free of it. Thus they evolved a science of special sounds—vibrations, which, when used properly, raise consciousness and break apart our deepest mental patterns. Mantras do have conceptual meaning, but their potency lies primarily in their vibrational impact. The old proverb, It takes a thorn to remove a thorn applies here. Introduction of a special thought (mantra) can cause the dismantling of a complex of other thoughts (core beliefs).

The mantras we are accustomed to come from Sanskrit, a sacred language from India. But every land has its sacred language, a language of prayer. Like a spiritual melody, mantras help to awaken our higher consciousness, beyond mind and ego. When the mind becomes still through the chanting of mantra, we connect again with the feeling of being loved and whole. In this way, we gradually become less bound by fixed patterns of thought and behavior.

The key to using a mantra for meditation is innocence. Just think it easily, with no effort, and if it starts to slip away, let it go. When you become aware that the mantra is no longer with you, just gently come back to it. The key is to expend no effort. As you repeat the mantra you can place your attention lightly at your heart.

The mantra will have the effect of gradually reducing your internal dialogue, so you don't want to concentrate on it or try and think about it. Use any mantra that feels intuitively right and repeat it silently to yourself with your eyes closed for twenty or thirty minutes each day. Or, you can repeat the mantra as you're drifting off to sleep.

As our internal dialogue is reduced, old thought patterns are spontaneously dismantled. Sometimes the dismantling can be quite intense, and we will experience an increase in mental activity for awhile. The key to meditation, as in everything else we've discussed in the book, is to accept whatever arises, including any thoughts or physical sensations. Consider such thoughts and sensations as purification, which is a positive benefit, rather than as anything special or wrong.

Here are some basic mantras that you may choose to use:

OM NAMAH SHIVAYA (she-veye-ya): The literal meaning of this mantra is "I surrender to the Lord."

RAM (rhymes with mom): This is another name for the Divine, which bestows peace, strength and compassion.

MA: This the first sound ever spoken. The ma mantra connects us to the Divine Mother, bringing love and nourishment.

SO'HAM (pronounced "so hum"): This is the natural sound of the ingoing and outgoing breath. *So* represents the feminine. *Ham* represents the masculine. In using this mantra, gently repeat So on the inhale and ham (pronounced "hum") on the exhale. Breathe naturally with no effort. Simply notice the breath as it enters and leaves the nostrils. After about ten minutes you will notice a quieting down of mental activity and softening of the breath. It happens effortlessly. Again, the key to meditation is freedom from effort.

Set aside a special time each day (twenty or thirty minutes to begin with), sitting comfortably and quietly with eyes closed, to meditate. Meditation is a vertical movement within, a movement out of time. (As opposed to analysis, which is horizontal, or a movement in time.) In meditation we don't want to analyze the experience, whether in the form of old memories, fleeting emotions, or creative ideas. The content of meditation is not the point. The point is to simply be. When the mind wanders off onto thoughts and we forget the mantra, we simply return to it when we become aware.

Chanting a mantra, silently or aloud, can be done while driving, sitting in a bus, gardening or during many other activities. The subconscious mind–the home of core beliefs—gradually gets infused with the mantra's healing vibration. Eventually the mantra will help dislodge our deepest habitual modes of thought.

Native American Indians and other indigenous cultures around the world have a long tradition of using special chants for healing and higher consciousness. Western psychology, on the other hand, is still relatively young in its mapping out of the human psyche. In its mechanistic approach to healing it has confined itself primarily to the realm of analysis and thought. These have their place, but until psychology affirms the Being—the impersonal Presence behind thought—it will remain superficial. Mantra takes us beyond thought. It helps to reconnect us to the deep silence of love, in the heart that we once experienced naturally as children.

A TEACHING FROM THE HOPI

In 1982, when our son, Julian, was barely four months old, we traveled to Hopi land in the Four Corners region of Arizona. While we were there, we attended a sacred fertility ceremony, the Hopi Snake Dance. Prior to the actual dance, old and young males live inside a *kiva*, a specially prepared cave with an entrance from the roof, along with many live, poisonous rattlesnakes. For many days and nights the boys, men, and snakes live together in the dark intimate womb of the kiva. Finally, reborn on the day of the ceremony, they strut outside into the sunlight and begin a circular dance around the plaza, turtle shells clacking from their ankles, striped snakes wrapped exquisitely around their red and white painted necks and ears. Everything is calm. Meditative. No thought. No fear. No attack. Only complete acceptance and love. The snakes and men are united in the dance of life.

How do they manage to cohabit with the poisonous snakes and not be bitten? We asked Grandfather David, who at that time was around 106 years old and the oldest of the tribe, their secret. He looked at us with a smile, pointed to Julian, and said, "Just like that . . . the way you love and care for your baby . . . soothing him, gently. This is how we treat the snakes . . . same way, same way. Only love." To live in love is to be free of our identification with thought.

When we enter the fire of love we must burn up our attachment to the rational mind. Love simply does not reside in the mind. Our relationship is at all times a perfect mirror of our relationship to ourselves. Our partners—like the characters in the Hopi Snake Dance—constantly reflect back to us the various archetypes of our inner reality. It is a gift to be both a mirror and reflection. In a spiritual partnership we always look to the lamp of awareness. When we find ourselves in conflict we look within while remaining open and present to our partners. Turning within makes us open, receptive. Now we can feel what has been denied perhaps our entire lives. As we grow in our ability to remain present, the feelings of pain and fear at the root of conflict eventually turn into the well-being of essence. It is here that our natural healing energies are fully awakened. Separation dissolves, and we find ourselves resting simply in the heart. Fear shifts to love. Guilt turns to gratitude. Our palms turn to the Beloved.

Love does not happen on the level of thought but in the calm acceptance of the heart. This calm acceptance is what we mean by the word *silence*. It is not actually the absence of thought but rather the absence of judgment. Just like the snakes, our agitated minds and bodies are not calmed by thought but by the kindness of a quiet heart. It is from this silence that we come to appreciate each other as the very embodiment of the Beloved. When we see the Beloved in one another all we can do is praise God for gifting us with the grace to see and feel beyond the limitations of the mind.

THE GOOD NEWS

It can be terrifying when we first attempt to undo our conditioned patterns of relating to each other. But the depth of our love can be a powerful catalyst for profound change and deep healing.

Often when there is a deep soul connection between partners, the ego undergoes a tremendous upheaval. Friends who were around when the two of us first got together thought we were absolutely crazy at times. And we were. The intensity of our love for each other was opening up all manner of repressed emotional energy. At first it was quite confusing. We had both been married previously and had had other relationships, but none before had ever catalyzed such emotional catharsis. The energy or shakti generated by our coming together opened us up physically, emotionally, mentally, and spiritually. Everything suppressed in childhood was released in the safety of each other's presence.

Eventually we realized that conflict does not necessarily indicate that something is wrong; it frequently accompanies growth and has to do with the stirring up of reactive patterns.

The good news is that with loving attention these patterns can be released, and your relationship can grow in joy. From this perspective, there is no need to suppress feelings or to judge. Conflict is part of the healing process and should be embraced as a fiery teacher.

This is a jumping off point in our investigation of the *Invisible Wedding*. In Part Two, Uniting with the Beloved, we explore in depth the spiritual realms of relating, including the merging of *chakras* and sacred sex. In the next chapter we introduce the Eastern concepts of *shakti* and *Tantra* and discover that, at the level of the heart, the forces of body and spirit are one.

Uniting with the Beloved

CHAPTER SIX

Shakti

Energy is eternal delight.
—William Blake

Most couples who make the journey into conscious relating eventually discover that their relationship has deeply significant spiritual overtones. The yoga of love can become a potent vehicle by which to transcend our duality, our primal feelings of separateness. In transcendent love we catch glimpses of the heart as it truly is, unencumbered, complete and whole. Over time, as our spiritual partnership flourishes, we find our love for each other reinforces our love for the Beloved. Indeed, as duality dissolves we notice that everything we encounter is the Beloved

As we have explored in previous chapters, once the focus on transformation intensifies, our partners become exquisite mirrors through which all the various aspects of our hidden inner selves get revealed, reflected, and contemplated. The dance between these varied facets of ourselves can be fiery yet profoundly liberating. But it is not only our shadows that dance. We also begin to dance with a highly creative and joyful spiritual force.

At a certain point early in our relationship, the two of us realized that since all of life is about relationship, why not relate with each other in a way that serves our spiritual freedom rather than the perpetuation of our suffering? Why not strive to become conscious partners? Why not see our relationship as a path to open the heart for soulful integration? How might the quality of our daily interactions shift were we to recognize the Beloved not only in a picture of Buddha, Jesus, or some other incarnation but here and now in the eyes of our partner? Such questioning proved a powerful turning point for us, and a spiritual partnership was born. Although there was little thought involved, the decision to follow a spiritual path as lovers and partners made itself obvious.

A spiritual partnership is a way of celebrating our love with such intensity and purpose that the binding affect of our separate egos dissolves, and our hearts become gradually infused with the nectar of unity. Devotion to our partner, to what he or she represents spiritually, softens the heart and gradually opens the inner doorway to the Beloved. We must have a passion for essential truth to walk such a road together. Spiritual partnership is a choice to realize love and is thus a challenge to anything in life that would cause us to close ourselves off to truth. Becoming spiritual partners means that we arrive at the understanding that the real Beloved is discovered within our own hearts, not in anything or anyone outside. However, this is not to diminish the wonder of relationship! A spiritual partnership—as we have explored throughout *The Invisible Wedding*—is a powerful catalyst for this awakening.

What Is Shakti?

The Taoist and Yoga scriptures of the Far East describe a particular vitalizing energy that we tap into as we awaken spiritually. This energy is called shakti. During sexual intercourse shakti is the heightened creative energy of fusion. Shakti is what heals and transforms our lives when we engage in spiritual practices such as meditation, chanting, prayer, and yoga. We also tap into shakti through dance, poetry, painting, music and creative work in general. When couples have the experience of genuinely falling in love, it is the shakti, the spiritual energy awakened internally, that starts to dance. This is the incredible ecstasy that lovers describe, the nectar that blissfully intoxicates us and boots us out of our rational minds. Shakti is the unifying spiritual force that flows throughout all creation. It is received by the heart as we open to life. We taste it in moments of ecstasy, in meditation or work, when the mind is still, when the tongue praises the Beloved, and anytime duality dissolves.

In many spiritual teachings of the Far East, shakti is the doorway to God, symbolized in the creative spark of womanhood, motherhood and Goddess worship. This is the Divine Feminine. Without shakti no creation can exist. Yet it also lives within males. Shakti is beyond gender, but we must become receptive to embrace it, thus the connection to the feminine principle. The Indian author Ajit Mookerjee describes it this way in the book *Kali:*

Shakti is the Power that creates and destroys,
the womb from which all things proceed and
to which all things return.

Shakti is the basic desire of the universe to create. It is the shakti that manifests in all varieties of plant, animal and human life, as well as that of planets, stars, solar systems, galaxies, and universes. Shakti is that which animates existence. At the basis of all life forms—whether animate or inanimate— is the desire to live and evolve. Mother Shakti (as She is referred to in India) manifests as pure creative desire. She is the life-force that runs through our veins, pumps our hearts, and inspires our thoughts. Shakti is the spirit of wholeness manifested in all living things. In the Christian charismatic movement shakti manifests as the Holy Spirit.

When we fall in love our desire is ignited. This extraordinary energy that we feel when we're in love is an aspect of shakti. Because it manifests as a sense of wholeness, it is akin to the Beloved.

Like many new lovers, when we fell in love we hardly slept for weeks. We were tapping into a source of erotic energy that seemed to have no end; the deeper we let go, the more of it we experienced. Having engaged in spiritual practices for many years, it became clear that we were connecting with the same shakti that awakens in meditation. As our relationship evolved, this intensely healing energy began mirroring back to us our various inner states of mind. We started getting in touch with deeper aspects of ourselves, and at times, as old pain resurfaced, the process was excruciating. At other times our experience of feeling shakti was sheer off-the-wall joy. Granted, joyfulness is nothing new in love. But this time *awareness* had also come into play. Somehow, by the grace of this shakti, we began to see that our relationship to each other pointed to a more essential one—with the Beloved. Our relationship to one another was not an end in itself, but a way to God—and a gift from God to help remove the thorn of separation from our hearts. It was a catalyst for expanding love. We began opening up not just with each other but to life as a whole. It was like stepping out of a cocoon, and donning colorful wings. Our love for one another reinforced our love of God.

The same Higher Power that years earlier had brought us to eyes-closed meditation now gave us the gift of each other. Our spiritual eyes were opened in a whole new way. The yoga of relating was at least as potent—if not more so—than that of meditation. This new path was about integration *into* life, not retreat from it. Our relationship was the perfect complement to the silence cultivated in eyes-closed meditation. The silence tapped in meditation was finally being integrated in activity, in the realm of relating. The shakti generated by our love was the vehicle for our coming home to the Beloved.

Through the study of Eastern spiritual texts we learned that there was a traditional teaching that pointed to the path of spiritual partnership on which we now found ourselves. It is called *Tantra*, and it is thousands of years old.

EVERYTHING IS HOLY

Tantra—an ancient body of spiritual knowledge from India—teaches that everything in creation is holy. Western seekers have focused primarily on the sexual aspect of Tantric teachings, but Tantra is really about wholeness. According to Tantra, sexual communion can be a means of self-realization when approached in a sacred way.

Tantra points to the interconnectedness of opposites. By putting Tantric teachings into practice, we can become attuned to both our inner feminine and inner masculine natures through sexual intimacy. In other words, through Tantric practice, a man unites with his inner female, and a woman joins with her inner male.

The whole universe is a play of opposites: the dance of electrons and protons; the turning of day into night, of one season into the next; the contrast of earth and sky, fire and water; the delicate balance of sodium and potassium in our bodies; the logical and intuitive hemispheres of the brain. And nowhere is the play of opposites more obvious than in the erotic dance between man and woman.

Spiritual wholeness can be defined as a co-existence of opposites. Within every male is an inner female archetype, a Venus grounding him to Sacred Earth and Her dark, moist mysteries. Within every woman is an inner male archetype, an Apollo supporting her movement toward Illumined Mind. Tantra teaches us that in the alchemy of intimate relating—which may or may not include sexual intercourse—we become conscious of our inner opposites. This is the reason we sometimes use the term "yoga of relationship" to describe this process. Yoga means union. As we unite sexually, emotionally, physically, and spiritually with our partners, we are actually reconnecting to the opposite archetypes within us that they represent. And in this way we become more balanced, and whole.

It is from this understanding of wholeness that Tantric teachings state that human consciousness contains the entire universe. The ancient Indian scripture, the *Mahanirvana Tantra*, declares: In truth, *every body is the universe!* This is simply a way of stating that we are whole; we are woven together of both feminine and masculine, yin and yang principles. A man's unconscious contains the feminine and is reflected in his relationship to his female partner. A woman's unconscious contains the masculine and is reflected in her relationship to her male partner. In this way, the harmony or tension we experience with our partner is a perfect mirror of the harmony or tension we experience inside us. This is why, during times of conflict, we are first asked to look within for the cause, instead of outward toward our partners. Our relationship will always reflect the deeper connection to ourselves. It is generally recognized that women, by nature, tend to nurture the values of relationship. Tantra is, at the most practical level, a teaching about relationship and how to live in harmony with our loved ones and the world at large. Thus, Tantra is traditionally associated with the worship of Shakti, the Goddess.

TANTRA AND THE DIVINE FEMININE

The ancient connection between Tantra and Goddess worship is in their honoring of the feminine—Nature, with its cycles of birth, growth, and decay; the body and sexuality; purification and healing; instinct and intuition; and visionary, holistic, and nonrational states of consciousness. In the earliest cultures, spirituality was never divorced from the body and the natural world. It was only as the world's societies (including those which gave us the Bible) embraced patriarchy that feminine values—and women themselves—were suppressed, dishonored, and diminished. Spiritual teachings that taught the sacredness of all life went underground, and the teachers were often persecuted and killed. The masculine/feminine energies underwent divorce. Mind separated from body. Humans separated from Nature, seeking domination rather than cooperation. Divine Mother worship disappeared into the solitude of mountains, forests, and jungles. Today, feminine values are returning, and the tear between the masculine and feminine is slowly being mended.

This teaching of spiritual partnership is not about matriarchy over patriarchy. It is not about gender. The adoration of the Divine Feminine simply has to do with restoring the status of the heart. From the heart we honor the body as a temple of God. We honor our relationship as a symbolic expression of the masculine/feminine powers at the basis of life. We appreciate the elements of fire, earth, air, water, and Nature itself as the Mother that gives us birth and sustains our journey through life until death. Tantra literally means "to weave." In the yoga of relationship, by being present for each other in all the ways discussed in previous chapters, we weave together the opposites of yin and yang, soft and firm, rational and intuitive, light and dark, conscious and unconscious, into a pattern of wholeness. Tantric teachings point to this wholeness of consciousness. Shakti is the spiritual energy that supports fusion and integration.

As we go deeper in our understanding of shakti and spiritual partnership, it can be helpful to explore the chakras, and how they open as our bond evolves. We will touch on them briefly now, and then go into greater detail in the next chapter.

SPIRITUAL GATEWAYS

Chakras are portals through which primal energy (shakti) materializes. There are seven such portals or points of energy, and each corresponds to a specific area of the body along the spinal column. The chakras are intimately involved in the regulation of the endocrine system. They also correspond to various psychological stages of development, from the most elementary impulses of survival and the formation of self-identity, to the loftiest heights of divine realization and the experience of Unity.

In childhood, when we live in an unconscious state of wonder, our chakras are partially open. This is the natural beauty, acceptance, and innocence we see in a very young child. As the ego develops and we move out of the heart and into the rational mind, causing fear to take hold, we shut down energetically—our chakras close—and we lose touch with our spiritual core. The nostalgia that many adults sometimes have for childhood has to do with wanting to be open again to life. We long for the time when we felt spiritually connected, when our chakras were open and shakti flowed effortlessly in our bodies.

Traditional ways of opening and developing our chakras as adults include meditation, fasting, prayer, yoga, devotion to God, and spiritual partnership (including sexual communion). As we discussed earlier, falling in love involves an intense rush of shakti. The flow of shakti and the opening of the chakras happen simultaneously. Our hearts, minds, and bodies light up with energy and, not unlike during childhood, we feel remarkably connected and turned on inside. Though most couples are unconscious of the process, the opening of our chakras is intimately connected to the bonding in our relationship. As we consciously open to each other—which, in a long-term relationship, includes times of emotional clearing and healing—our chakras also open together. Shakti increases in this way, and the split inside between the masculine and feminine is healed. In uniting with our partners we are, in effect, mending our true relationship with the Beloved.

In a spiritual marriage we bond not just on the physical and emotional levels, but in each of the seven chakras. In the next chapter we will utilize the conceptual framework of the chakras as a map for further exploring this path of unity through spiritual partnership.

CHAPTER SEVEN

Union

Whose idea was this,
to have the lover visible,
and the Beloved invisible?
—RUMI

The principle of synergy—the whole being greater than the sum of the parts—provides a key in understanding the transformative nature of a spiritual partnership. When we come together to share in a generous, heart-filled love of life, a powerful transformative energy is generated. We find the potential to bond at each of the seven chakras. The apparent gap between self and other will start to close, and a fullness will grow that is greater than what either of us experience alone. This is the spiritual secret behind the devotional path to marriage. We unite with each other not just physically, but emotionally, mentally, and spiritually as well.

Let us investigate each chakra and how we align as partners within each one.

ALIGNING OUR FIRST CHAKRAS: SURVIVAL

The first chakra at the base of the spine is considered the store-house of shakti and is considered the root of consciousness. Psychologically, this center has to do with patterns of survival, fear, possessiveness, food, and money. When we experience "losing our ground," or find ourselves "spaced out," we are often disconnected from this root chakra.

In the process of aligning our root chakras, we naturally be-come aware of issues relating to survival and security. At the surface this often translates into our relationship with money. At the emotional level we face the fear of loss. At the deepest level, we encounter the reality of death. Until we experience that nothing is permanent and that death is an ally, the heart cannot fully open.

As the intimacy intensifies between us and greater shakti — that is, energy and awareness—awakens, the fears or hidden agendas that exist unconsciously in our relationship will start to emerge. Are we attached to each other primarily for secu-rity? Do we rely on each other more than God? Is our love at all financially based? Are we using money as a way of control-ling our partners? Are we afraid to speak our truth for fear of losing the relationship? Certain conventional relationships work quite well when they are negotiated like a business, but spiritual partnerships inevitably confront deeper questions and consequently drive us into the core of the heart. In a con-ventional or more unconscious relationship, such material is often suppressed. Various strategies of avoidance and denial are woven into relating, which results in a mutual shutting down of the potential energy of our root chakras. Such a relationship is often based on fear, not love, and will eventually die spiritually, if not physically.

By contrast, in a spiritual partnership we welcome whatever discomfort arises. We do not hide from ourselves or each other. We view our fear not as something to be denied but to be embraced as a messenger of insight into our separateness and the need to return to a sense of union in love. We cooperate by tuning into the sensation of fear in our bodies. We challenge hidden negative core beliefs and affirm our essential union. In this way our intimacy continually deepens, and our creative energy, which is no longer bound up in fear, is consumed in love. The power of love—shakti—at the level of the first chakra seeks to consume our survival issues.

To help move into alignment in the first chakra, we can begin to bridge whatever separation might exist with regard to finances. Although each relationship is unique, there are several general principles that help couples to align in this way. One is to merge your finances as efficiently as possible. Separate bank accounts do not facilitate spiritual bonding. Instead, we teach the elegant principle of unlimited sharing. We hold nothing back from each other.

We worked recently with a couple in an intense first chakra struggle. Although both partners contributed significantly to the well-being of the family, the man was the primary breadwinner. Somehow, he felt this entitled him to be the primary financial decision maker as well. His wife was expected to account for every dollar she spent. As you can imagine, this became the source of tremendous strife in their marriage. It reflected a deep distrust between them and a separation inside their own hearts.

In any kind of conflict each person must look within. Control issues are symptomatic of unacknowledged fear. When communication finally opened up a bit for this particular couple both admitted a reluctance to let go of control for fear of abandonment. She was unwilling to rock the boat—to speak her truth—for fear that he would leave. He was unwilling to relax his grip on the money for fear that she would take advantage of greater financial freedom, and possibly find another partner. The issue was the same for both the husband and wife: Fear of loss. Facing our fears and sharing honestly with each other are essential to freeing up our spiritual energy. On the other hand, suppressing such root chakra issues robs a relationship of its vitality—of that powerful shakti that wants to flow between partners and nurture their connection.

We live in a culture that values power and financial status (masculine principles) over nurturing and loving kindness (feminine principles). But spiritual wisdom reveals that the partner who takes care of the home and nurtures the children contributes as much to a spiritual partnership as the partner who goes out to work each day. The at-home partner provides the spiritual manna, the shakti, for the income-earning partner to manifest his or her talents in the outside world. When a couple recognizes this truth and begins to balance their root level chakras, new sources of energy, joy and vitality are discovered.

As couples let go of their respective fears, a deep sense of well-being arises. Shakti flows abundantly, and the material needs of the household are met with increasing ease and comfort. We discover that it is actually from the substance of our love that our needs are met. The quiet presence of our devotion, like an invisible magnet, seems to attract what is needed materially, emotionally and spiritually.

Here are some simple procedures for dismantling negative patterns related to the root chakra.

1. Join Your Finances Whenever Possible—Make available to each other any private, protected source of savings and income. Decide together how you will manage the finances and what each partner's role will be.

2. Discuss Any Emotional Fears or Insecurities—Work together on feeling free to explore such issues. For example, does the fear of abandonment surface when you consider your economic situation? Do you become anxious over your financial conditions? Is there a fear of betrayal connected to money matters?

3. Meditate—Find the space inside that is unspoiled by thought. Fear boils down to a lack of faith in God and a belief that we are in control of our life. Through meditation the conscious mind gets attuned to the only power that truly knows the way.

4. Affirm Your Union—Work with the following affirmation: "We are one with God, the Source of infinite energy, wisdom, and compassion. God supports our union. Nothing can happen that isn't meant to happen."

Aligning Our Second Chakras: Sexual

The second chakra is located behind the genitals. When shakti awakens here, it affects our sexuality, passion and creativity. This is the easiest place to come to an understanding of shakti. We all know what it is like to get turned on. Sexual energy is simply shakti dancing in the second chakra.

Psychological patterns connected to this center have to do with self-worth, self-esteem, and self-identity. Those of us having undergone any kind of sexual abuse and not having had the opportunity to heal will experience deep blocks in this chakra. Being harshly criticized or disrespected as a child will also have a negative impact. Promiscuity, inhibition, difficulty in establishing appropriate boundaries, fear of intimacy, and low self-worth involve negative conditioning related to our sexuality. Also, wounding in the sexual chakra often causes the shutting down of all the other chakras, particularly the heart. Aligning our second chakras eventually involves the healing of previous sexual wounds, as the unifying power of love purifies such injuries.

As couples merge more deeply at the sexual chakra, wounds from the past can arise. The dramatic increase in shakti and the dissolving of defenses brings our suppressed wounds to the surface, resulting in a healing crisis that we will need to address as spiritual partners. What are some of the issues that might arise?

Here Are Some Issues that Could Arise During a Healing Crisis.

- A woman who was abused either sexually or emotionally as a teenager might find her body tightening up as she and her partner enter into deeper levels of sharing.

She might find herself resisting a more intense sexual or emotional intimacy.

- A man who is not in touch with his feminine side might be conditioned to take a dominant role in lovemaking. He might therefore find himself becoming uncomfortable when his less inhibited partner takes a more active role in their sexual play.

- A man or woman who feels the compulsive need to be with sexual partners other than his or her mate may have suffered sexual abuse in the past. The affairs are a defense mechanism to help avoid the pain that comes with real intimacy. Since intimacy between deeply connected spiritual partners stirs up wounds from our past, those who can't face confronting those wounds might be tempted to exchange sexual energy with a less committed partner.

A spiritual partnership can be a powerful context for working through such sexual issues. Healing from a sexual wound and aligning our second chakras require that partners not only give each other respect, compassion, and love, but that they fully trust each other and have faith in the Beloved. With these elements in place, they can eventually let down their defenses, open up to each other, and experience authentic intimacy. The more we can freely open ourselves to our spiritual partner, the deeper our healing—and our connection.

Emotional detachment during lovemaking, avoidance of intimacy, premature ejaculation, inability to orgasm, and general distrust are often indicative of some blockage in our sexual chakras. Again, the beauty of a spiritual partnership is that it can provide the depth and care needed to explore our healing. It is deeply reassuring to know that we are not going to be abandoned or judged as we open to a partner whom we deeply trust. Being held in the arms of our beloved as we reveal our most tender wounds is a healing gift beyond words.

We recently had a woman visit us, who, in the midst of healing her sexual abuse as a child, found it necessary to temporarily abstain from sex with her husband. She was simply too vulnerable. She communicated her worry to us that it wasn't fair to him. What will he do for the next few months? Will he get angry? Will he find another partner? Will he have an affair? Yet when she discussed the matter with her husband, the gift became obvious to both of them. Here was an opportunity for the husband to show support for his wife at a most delicate period in their lives.

He shared with us how, over their sixteen years of marriage, she had nurtured him through some of the toughest times of his life. She had been there for him during job changes, loss of confidence, and illness. Helping his wife to heal at this chakra level gave him the chance to learn how to do something very important: to give freely without the need to receive anything in return. Giving selflessly in this way not only strengthened his bond with his wife, it proved as important for his own healing as for hers.

Most couples have some degree of blockage in their sexual chakras. If we are to deepen our spiritual partnership, we cannot avoid our sexuality anymore than we can deny our heart connection to the Beloved.

We worked with a couple who made their initial appointment with us because of what they believed was a sexual performance difficulty. It seems the man would ejaculate almost the moment he entered his partner. What technique, they wondered, could they learn to remedy his premature ejaculation? It was evident to us that the problem was not sexual—it almost never is. It was an issue of the heart.

Over the next few weeks we guided them into an exploration of their emotional connection. What was it inside his partner that frightened this man? She was a strong, vivacious woman, highly successful in real estate. He was an investment broker who, over the last couple years, had experienced some major setbacks in his career. He began to interpret his failure at work as a lack of his value as a human being. The fact that his wife was so proficient in her field intensified his feelings of inadequacy.

As we mentioned earlier, self-worth issues are intimately tied to our second chakras. Doubting himself as a man resulted in the shutting down of this individual's sexual energies. Reaching an intense level of intimacy with his wife became too much to bear, as it exposed his feelings of insufficiency. Premature ejaculation became an unconscious method of preventing contact with his wife, and thus a way to avoid the deeper issue of self-acceptance and love.

Once this gentleman was able to completely face into his underlying feelings of inadequacy, his premature ejaculation ceased. This process of "facing into" the inadequacy pattern, however, was more than simply talking about it. He had to clearly see—and feel—the predicament of having identified himself too narrowly with work-related success and failure. His self-acceptance was high when he experienced success, low when he experienced failure. Where is the equanimity in such a yo-yo state of mind? Where was his center? It was obviously externalized. But the appearance of failure, both at home and at work, was a blessing in disguise as it forced this man to acknowledge being overly identified with a standard of happiness outside himself. Slowly, he began the journey of seeing that he was whole regardless of external circumstances. And realizing this, he saw that he didn't need to perform to feel loved.

These crucial insights allowed this individual to open sexually to his partner at an entirely new level of experience. Letting go of his attachment to what he thought he was —and to the obsessive need to perform in the world—allowed him to relax, which made him more receptive to and aware of his partner and their sexual bonding. He was more fully present—and his heart was more open.

His wife had to investigate her own heart as well. Questions arose: Did she carry any judgment of her husband for his "lesser" achievements? Did she have a need to compare her performance to his? What was it inside her that might have scared or intimidated her husband? Was she safe with him? Was she safe with her inner male? Was she able to comfortably receive her husband and consequently deepen her receptivity?

As couples, our patterns are complementary, fitting together like a lock and key. The potency of sexual intercourse especially magnifies the emotional/psychic energy between us. As the woman's attention turned toward herself, she faced the part inside that had been almost business-like toward her husband. He was like another competitor. Someone she felt she had to top in some way. She saw that over the years of achievement in the business world she had sacrificed her feminine nature—that part of herself that was tender, open, and receptive. This tied into her childhood and the need to perform well in order to receive approval and acceptance from her parents. She was indeed judgmental of her husband. It now became clear that the judgment she felt toward him for his business failures arose from her own insecurity. His apparent failure, which extended even to the bedroom, was a reflection of the hidden part of her that felt like a failure. And this sense of inner failure was at the root of her overly masculinized approach to life.

With these insights, this woman's heart began to open, and the love and approval she had sought outwardly through her career achievements started to awaken internally. As she felt inwardly more whole as a woman, she naturally became more receptive toward her husband. Both felt safer in each other's presence. And the sexual dance deepened and intensified between them as each brought more fullness to the relationship.

When we heal the separateness inside we begin to appreciate others not as objects but as intimate parts of ourselves, the one heart with which we dance, celebrate, and enjoy life. Sex becomes truly healing and transformative when joined with the heart.

Here are some essential points to aligning sexual chakras.

1. Release Notions of Sex as a Prerequisite to Love—Women (primarily) must let go of the notion of having to engage in sex to be loved. Feeling that we have to give our bodies away in order to be loved creates abuse, not love. The deepest truth is simply that we are love, independent of what we think, say, or do.

2. Overcome the Impulse to Perform—Men (primarily) must understand the root feeling behind the need to perform generates fear, which causes tension and a lack of sensitivity to our partners. Feeling obliged to perform does not allow us just to be but rather creates a separation between our mind and body. We can dissolve this pattern by regular meditation and by understanding that we are whole as we are, independent of what we think, say, or do. When we bring inner silence into lovemaking, we become open, receptive, relaxed, and passionate.

3. Set Aside Time to Share—Arrange a special sharing time (not during or immediately before sex) for discussing resentments or secrets that might be preventing your hearts (and bodies) from opening fully.

Sometimes, when there is confusion or dilemma in a couple's sexuality, we recommend that they build a fire—either separately or together. Each person writes down their sexual histories, including the names of past lovers, and throws the paper into the fire as a symbolic gesture of purification and letting go. Share whatever you feel is preventing an opening between you. The important thing is to write down any secrets or sexual difficulties and give it to the fire. This exercise cleanses the subconscious and supports our alignment at the second chakra.

4. Be Simple, Honest and Forthright—Faith in each other's integrity allows for the deepest possible union. Sexual betrayal can be extraordinarily painful and complicated. On the one hand, it usually involves deceit toward our mates, and on the other it often turns another into an object for personal satisfaction. Both factors reinforce our separateness and cause suffering.

Agreements between partners can change, but when it comes to an issue as potent as sex, decisions must never be made unilaterally. Both your own heart and your partner's must be carefully and compassionately consulted.

There can be circumstances in life when a deep and profound soul connection happens with someone outside our primary partnership. A deep love for another individual is by no means neurotic or pathological, nor is it a real threat to a mature relationship, but it can be challenging. When a relationship with someone other than our primary partner upsets the harmony between us, we must ask our hearts: Does this relationship elevate the love between us and our family? Are we enriched in some fundamental way? Are both of us supported? Is it truly a soul connection? If a new relationship does not add to the harmony in our primary one, if our capacity for love is not expanded, it is best to walk away. Only the ego will struggle with our decision. Looking into your hearts together will strengthen the alignment between you and deepen the unity of your hearts, minds, and bodies.

When a sexual need arises outside the context of our primary relationship, we must look within ourselves to determine why it is happening. What is our real need here? Is it love, or is it simply lust? Perhaps it is a call for greater intimacy with our partner. Perhaps there is a need to go deeper into our spirituality. The arising of sexual desire for someone other than our partner is rarely about love, regardless of what our minds tell us at the time. It's also important to realize that all desire does not have to be acted on. Sitting with strong desire can become an intense fire (in India it is called *tapas*) in which our attention is driven to the very core of our apparent cravings and wanting. Such containment of desire can become a part of spiritual practice.

At the deepest level, desire for sex is often a disguise for a desire for union with the Beloved. In the context of a spiritual partnership, where loyalty and love of God is mutual, sex can indeed open the inner door. But when we follow through on a casual physical attraction, our spiritual awareness is dragged down, rather than elevated.

So what role does monogamy play in a spiritual partnership? When our sexual energy is contained, the shakti generated by our devotion to one person strengthens the union between us at the deepest levels. Sexual exclusivity becomes a vehicle for clearing out subconscious blocks and transcending primal duality. All the energy centers get enlivened as we merge with one another at the deepest levels of sexual intimacy. In this sense, monogamy can be a way of growing in unity consciousness. This does not happen with casual sex.

Part of what defines a spiritual partnership is the courage to face ourselves and one another in the deepest, most authentic way. Some agreements between us, like who pays the bills or takes out the garbage, can be changed quite easily. Others, like those involving sexual boundaries are very delicate and must not be changed without serious reflection. This is because the exchange of sexual energy has enormous impact on our physical bodies and spiritual selves. It potentially opens the heart and nurtures harmony and bonding at the deepest, subtlest levels. Sex can get complicated if deep unconscious energies are awakened in a context outside our primary relationship. And certainly the balance can be thrown off center between us if a third partner is brought into the picture. For most of us who are intent on growing spiritually together, a monogamous relationship is the simplest path.

5. Release All Guilt Based on Sex—Let go of any guilt associated with your sexuality, no matter what you've done, are doing, or have thought about doing. As powerful as guilt is, it is not an effective deterrent to illicit behavior. Falling in love with someone other than your partner; lusting after your neighbor when his wife is in the hospital; promiscuity out of a need for love, such things are as old as marriage. Naturally, we do not place such experiences in the plus column, and their consequences are often severe. But they happen because unconsciously we need those experiences for growth. In some incomprehensible way they advance the plot of life. Some people become humbled enough to turn within through such experiences. Others can't let go of the guilt, which is the ego's way of perpetuating the judged behavior. At one level, guilt is a way of repeating the action as a way of self-punishment. At a deeper level, guilt is the seeking of forgiveness so that we can again feel innocence.

From our perspective, such predicaments are a call to listen more deeply to the heart. It is more fruitful to investigate the roots of our unconscious patterns and ponder what might want to be fulfilled, than torment ourselves with guilt and shame.

ALIGNING OUR THIRD CHAKRAS: CONTROL AND FEELINGS

The third chakra is the energy center approximately associated with the navel. Physically it involves our digestive system, particularly the spleen, liver, and pancreas. Psychologically it has to do with issues of authority, control, power, jealousy, attachment and enthusiasm. This is also the emotional center; thus it is connected with a certain level of feeling. This is where the term "gut feeling" arises.

One need only ponder the vast numbers of Americans, especially males, suffering from various forms of stomach upset such as gastritis and ulcers to realize how stuck we are at this level. Seen from the window of an unhealed third chakra, circumstances in life are a matter of proper control and manipulation. We embody a basic distrust for life; thus, we believe we must manipulate life to gain support.

Children who feel they must perform well to deserve love from the adults around them tend to grow up with tight third chakras. They become the overachievers and, in some cases, the underachievers. They learn how to meet their emotional needs by manipulating the circumstances around them, especially people. Is there any real intimacy at this level? Only when we learn to relax our bellies, to trust in a power bigger than ourselves, does life begin to work in a free-flowing and relaxed fashion. We learn to meet our true needs without having to employ control or manipulation.

The third chakra is also the source of much enthusiasm and vitality. Vitality arises with the gentle loosening of our bellies. Ever notice how, in the East, Buddha is sometimes depicted with a soft, round belly? This is indicative of his unworried, relaxed posture in life. As healing happens in the third chakra and shakti is free to flow at this level, we let go of control. We stop trying to push the river, allowing the events in our life to take their natural course.

When the third chakra opens through our intimacy with each other, we become aware of the powerful force behind our attachments, both to each other and to other things of the world. We begin to feel the fear that feeds our desire systems of wanting, achieving and possessing. We begin to recognize how our need for control is a way of maintaining our distance and avoiding emotional contact. Gradually, as we grow together in greater awareness, the subtle umbilicus that attaches us to unwholesome ways with one another begins dissolving. This corresponds to a softening of the belly center. Love blossoms when we let go of control and surrender to a higher will.

We have worked with many women over the years who felt that if they did not keep perfect homes and function in some successful capacity in the world, they did not deserve to be loved. Such women are continually trying to prove themselves around males. Control, more than love, was the binding force in the majority of their relationships. Behind such control is a core belief that we need to perform well to be loved because it is not enough to simply be ourselves. Control is always based on fear, which is based on the illusion of a separate self. Love, in contrast, is the absence of separation.

Men's third chakra issues often center around power and control in the outside world. Since so much of our culture is based on greed, competition and personal power, our value in the eyes of others as well as in our own is determined by our success or failure in the working world. Our culture glorifies material achievement, and many males have difficulty understanding that the qualities that go into achieving material success do not guarantee success in relating to one's partner or family. Love obeys a higher law. Personal drive might get you a new car or a raise at the office, but it cannot renew and sustain intimacy. When it comes to matters of the heart, qualities of cooperation and surrender take precedence over competition and personal power. Caring takes precedence over cunning. We cannot force a heart to open. We cannot will someone to love us without doing harm.

We know a doctor who receives the highest accolades from his peers and patients yet cannot bear the fire of intimate contact with his wife and children. His control switch is turned on from the moment he awakens to the time he crawls in bed some eighteen hours later. His children feel the constant need to achieve in order to receive his approval. His wife feels frustrated at the lack of emotional intimacy between them.

Control is always a mask for the need to feel loved. It arises from core beliefs that life does not support us, that we cannot get our needs met without force, that there is no higher power guiding and supporting us on our journey. As a result our bellies tighten, our shoulders knot up, and our hearts hunger for the joy of human love and affection.

Deep inside the heart and mind of this accomplished doctor is a little child who longs to be appreciated solely for who he is, not for how well he performs. Nothing can satisfy him, nothing can break his incessant need for control except the well-being that comes with feeling loved. Ultimately, behind his control is the fear that he is separate from the stream of life and that in letting down his guard his needs for love and security will not be met.

Jealousy is also a third chakra issue and can be one of the most difficult emotions to face. The root of jealously lies in the misperception that the source of love is outside us. How can we work with jealousy? We have to acknowledge it and then feel it. What we feel is the unbearable fear of loss behind our need for control. When we are able to remain open to the pain, we eventually understand that true love is based on freedom, not fear. There is no easy way to arrive at this insight except through the crucible of experience. The gift in jealousy is that we come face to face with the bald truth that we have absolutely no control over the people we love. A spiritual partnership is not based upon control, and so we must look within to dismantle jealousy, rather than trying to control our partner's behavior. With the loosening of our attachments—often out of the sheer anguish of the experience—we come to experience a new level of wholeness within.

Opening a blistered heart can be excruciating at times. Author and Buddhist teacher Ken McLeod writes in the book, *Wake Up to Your Life*, "A student asked Dingo Khyenste Rinpoche, 'Why do we practice?' He replied, 'To make the best of a bad situation.'" Jealousy is a bad situation, but it is made even worse by denying it.

The passionate shakti of love eventually brings to our awareness the places inside that we guard and protect. The mirror of our relationship makes it all too clear the ways we control and manipulate to avoid intimacy. Intimacy is about seeing into ourselves through the window of our lover's eyes. Control is a basic strategy for avoiding such close contact.

Our bellies are not only centers of control but of emotions as well—especially anger and fear, but also enthusiasm. People with relaxed guts are generally comfortable expressing feelings as they naturally arise. Look at a child's belly!

We remember our son Nathan when he was a toddler. He strutted around the house like a little king at times, shoulders naturally back, big round belly naturally extended. Feelings were immediate, and there was no holding back. He would request, "Just one more cookie," and when the request was turned down his eyes would suddenly well up in huge salty tears and his mouth would open wide in a loud, raucous scream. There was absolutely no doubt that in that moment Nathan was angry. Yet five minutes later Nathan's attention would be turned to a fleet of toy cars, and a new adventure would begin. His feelings of disappointment over the cookie would be washed clean like clear mountain water, leaving virtually no impression. At that stage of his life, Nathan was pure, unripened Buddha mind.

We have addressed the shadow side of our third chakras, yet there is also much light and creativity that flows through here as well. As we purify our third chakras, as we learn to trust in the flow of life, in a Higher Power, we act and respond toward life with a deeper sense of ease and generosity. With relaxed bellies we learn to take each day as it comes, losing the need to push the river or force circumstances to conform to our demands. Paradoxically, as we release our need for control, we seem to be given more of it. As we let go of our attachment to power, we seem to have it. As we let go of our attachment to outcomes, things adjust themselves more effortlessly in our favor. With a generous spirit we give to life, and life gives back. We become a blessing to our loved ones, and our loved ones— feeling at ease in our company—respond with love and affection. Shakti flows, hearts mend, and mountains move.

The fire of a conscious relationship requires us to let go of everything we are not so that we can dance in the awareness of what is. A relaxed belly means a big heart.

Let us now explore some perspectives on uniting our third charkas and the benefits that arise.

1. Reconcile Any False Gender Beliefs—Take a personal inventory of any erroneous beliefs you might hold concerning gender inequality. Be completely honest with yourself. Do you believe that women are inferior? Do you believe that men are inferior? The dualistic notion of superior/inferior arises from the mind's basic sense of separateness from life, and it is born of fear.

Share your insights with each other. As we challenge our belief in separation we become aware of the innumerable ways we have attempted to control the people and circumstances in our environment. We might also become conscious of a certain underlying tightness in our guts. This tension is a physical expression of our mind's faulty constructs.

2. Explore Negative Feelings Together—Be willing to explore together any withheld feelings of anger, resentment, sadness, and fear that might have accumulated over time. Our bellies are the cauldrons for any unhealed emotional baggage that we have been unable to let go of.

Sometimes we give clients the affirmation: My anger is my love! This can help to release any guilt that we might be carrying as the result of having so-called "negative feelings" such as anger. Anger becomes negative only when we cannot find the appropriate means of working with it. Sometimes we need to share it outright. Sometimes we need to find a quiet space and work with it meditatively using the breath and awareness. Either way, anger is not wrong; it just is.

The same holds true for any other feelings that want to arise. To be alive is to feel. Life does not discriminate between good and bad feelings. Life does not label the experience of fear as being worse than sadness. Fear is part of the human condition. Anger is part of being human. Sadness is part of being alive. Some grief is written into every love story. To feel is to be alive.

Spiritual partners become open, transparent. Expressing to our partner what we truly feel is a way of opening our hearts and revealing our vulnerability. Although it can be quite painful to stay truly present for our partner when he or she is giving expression to grievances, it is a powerful spiritual practice. Our inner reactions define the edges of our growth in the moment.

3. Increase Your Awareness of Each Other—Let go of "me" consciousness and start thinking from the more expanded perspective of "we." Think of your partner's needs before your own. This cultivates trust and a broader, more universal sense of self. A cramped third chakra, a tightened belly, tends to restrict our awareness of the other person. Choose the perspective that "we're in this together."

From the spiritual perspective, there is only one heart. What we offer to each other we offer to ourselves, or, more accurately, to the Beloved.

4. Open Your Mind to Another Point of View—Consciously give your partner the benefit of winning at an argument. There is nothing like letting go of the need to be right to open up a tight situation. Make a sincere effort to listen and understand your partner's opinion and perspective.

5. Practice Letting Go of Control—When you feel compelled to assume control simply relax and breathe deeply from the belly. Support your partner in fulfilling a strong desire she or he might hold, even when it requires you to stretch emotionally. To unite with one another at the third chakra is to relax into life and to acknowledge who is truly minding the store! The world has a distorted perception of love, relationship, and marriage. It is not about possession, control, or anything having to do with the conditioned mind. It is about acceptance of what is.

6. Allow Yourselves to Think Forbidden Thoughts—Better yet, break some social or psychological taboo occasionally, one that is relatively harmless. Thinking forbidden thoughts and breaking taboos can be powerfully catalytic. We often fail to appreciate how much energy is required to remain inside our tight conceptual boxes. Enormous control mechanisms surface when our thought or behavior counters what the dominant part of us holds as forbidden or taboo.

ALIGNING OUR FOURTH CHAKRAS: HEART

The center of the chest is considered the heart, or fourth chakra. As our love awakens at this point we begin to manifest such qualities as compassion, unconditional love, generosity, and in the transition from the third to fourth chakra, the shadow feelings of grief, fear and selfishness. America has a great heart but hides it under the cloak of tough rhetoric and an insatiable appetite for power and material security. Such tendencies are one factor in the proliferation of heart disease in this country. Chronic fourth chakra contraction can result in both lack of intimacy and heart disease.

As sensitive children, perhaps we had to shut down our hearts to keep from being exploited. Now as adults, we might find it difficult to break through the callousness of our defenses in order to be emotionally present and available for each other.

The heart chakra is considered the bridge between the lower animal and higher divine aspects. As humans, we encompass both. As the heart opens, third chakra issues around power and control are released; lust is transformed into love;

guilt gives way to forgiveness, jealousy becomes detachment. We no longer react to life from the primal survival instincts of our lower chakras. We see beyond the mask of personality. Love takes on a less personal, more unconditional nature. Life becomes more spontaneous and is witnessed. From this growing sense of the impersonal nature of things arises compassion.

When the heart begins opening we experience the subtle distinction between true feeling and emotion. Emotion, we begin to observe, is a kind of turbulence associated with our navel and solar plexus centers. Anger, rage, guilt, jealousy and envy are classic emotions experienced in the pit of our stomachs; they tend to reinforce our sense of separateness. Yet at a subtler level (or at a higher octave in the heart) these same emotions get transmuted into other kinds of feelings, which, rather than separating us from each other and our environment, somehow connect us more strongly. Feeling—as distinguished from raw emotion—joins us to the stream of life. Fear gives way to feeling connected. Jealousy relaxes into a sense of security and spaciousness. Guilt transforms into an acceptance of things as they are. Feeling at this depth brings compassion and an inclination to reduce suffering. Feeling born out of an open heart sends out a deep caring into the world allowing us to appreciate others in terms of the Beloved. The walls that divided us before are no longer experienced. The opening and aligning of the heart chakra is about acceptance.

It is really here at the heart center that unhealthy modes of competition die and the pure experience of cooperation and service arise effortlessly. It is from the heart that we begin to appreciate a real sense of unity. Such connectedness is beyond the mind. Marriage now becomes a reflection of the true Inner

Wedding. It does not come, however, without going through the ordeal of facing into all that separates us.

Purification of the heart often begins with a painful awareness of the ways in which we have learned to close ourselves off from life and each other. We become aware of our selfishness, hatred, intolerance, and of the cramping down of our heart. Fear is the shadow side of love, and thus it is no surprise that as the heart opens we initially become aware of just how terrified we are to be fully alive, open, and trusting. From such a fearful space the desire to give is often motivated by a need to receive. When we do give, we give certain things but never our hearts.

We hesitate to respond to a neighbor's needs for fear of involvement. What if our hearts are touched and we share in their suffering? We come to see how the ego's emphasis is always on control, on a continuous neurotic search for personal satisfaction, which, paradoxically, we never truly experience until we forget ourselves.

Jesus was perhaps the ultimate heart master. When asked how many times a person should give his coat to another in need, He replied, "Seventy times seven"! When confronting an angry mob stoning the prostitute Mary Magdalene he said, "He who is without sin cast the first stone"! And, of course, He also taught that it is more blessed to give than to receive. Christ was speaking from his natural state of awareness resting in the heart.

Our teacher Ammachi, from India, is a modern day Christ. She radiates such love and compassion in a gathering that thousands of people are struck to the core by Her presence. We have watched Her caress lepers, people dying of aids, the homeless, and others all night long, without any apparent thought of Her

own fatigue or physical condition. Amma's love is unconditional. Her heart has fully flowered. She is uniting the world in
love, one warm hug at a time.

Here are some tips for aligning at the heart chakra.

1. Practice Choosing Love Over Fear—How does this work
in an everyday situation? Let's say your partner is tired and
gets upset over the fact that you forgot to pick up milk on the
way home from work. He or she might fire at you: "You always forget to do what I ask you—obviously you don't care
about what goes on around here!" The remarks sting you,
only this time instead of reacting from old conditioning, you
choose to see beyond surface appearances.

Shifting from your reactive position to your heart chakra,
you can appreciate how your partner feels. You realize that no
positive solution can come out of such intensity of emotion;
therefore, you curb your tendency to fight back and instead
find a way to support your partner. You might say something
like, "You are absolutely right. What can I do to help you
out?" Such a response—when genuine—comes from a choice
to be in our hearts rather than our emotionally reactive guts.
We choose love over fear, peace over conflict. When you
choose this path you'll likely find that after a few minutes
your partner will soften up and apologize for the distressed
outburst. He or she might disclose that what they really want
is reassurance of your love, not the gallon of milk.

There is a beautiful saying in the *Course In Miracles* that deals
with conflict. It says, in essence, that we are never upset for the
reason we think we are. The next time your partner blows up at
you because you forgot to pick up the laundry or didn't cook

the chicken properly, see if there isn't a deeper distress. You can communicate to him or her that their rage is misplaced and unacceptable yet still choose to see their essential innocence. Each time we respond with love, which is a choice to see beyond surface appearances, we open and align with one another at the heart chakra. Fear is released—and love grows.

2. Openly Express Love and Appreciation—In the transi tion period between the third and fourth chakras remember to out-wardly demonstrate your love and appreciation for each other. Many layers of suppressed fear and hurt come to the surface as part of the purification. We need to be gentle with each other. Couples in long-term relationships often begin taking for granted each other's company and support. In a spiritual part-nership love is nothing if not manifested. There are many ways to demonstrate our love. Here are just a few:

- Stop by a florist on the way home and pick up a dozen of your partner's favorite flowers. This gesture tells her or him that they are cherished by you.
- Schedule regular one-on-one fun time together. Take turns choosing a particular enjoyable activity to engage in. Support each other in your decision.
- Give each other massages. Nothing communicates better than touch. Nothing heals like touch. Making love is wonderful after a massage, so long as you both desire it and it is based on giving. Whatever the focus, it must re-main on giving.
- Give each other an occasional break from household chores. Take turns preparing food or, if you have young children, putting them to bed.

3. Pace Your Sexual Energy—When making love, shift the attention up from the genitals directly into the heart. Keep the awareness on the heart as the bliss between you intensifies. Gently resist the tendency to orgasm quickly. Stay present for each other. Learning to channel our sexual energy is a powerful tool for opening up our chakras. Let it be natural, unhurried, and unforced.

4. Embrace Your Emotions Together—Take time each week to share any feelings that may be arising for you. Sometimes the greatest gift you can give each other is simply listening. When we truly communicate with one another, the heart opens and warm feelings of love flow. There is tremendous healing power in the ability to remain unguarded while receiving feedback. Both hearts are healed in the process. When a grievance is shared, assume that the feedback is arising from a positive place, from a desire to support you and the relationship. Learn to emotionally embrace whatever arises within you.

There is a liberating quality to truth. The Biblical saying that the Truth shall set you free has meaning on many levels. In our relationship, it is important to express ourselves in a way that supports the well-being of our partners. As the heart opens further, our speech and behavior quite naturally reflect a higher quality of truth and harmony.

5. Recognize Endearing Attributes—Praise your partner for his or her strengths and kindnesses. Praise is the language of the heart and, at its root, is the simple acknowledgment of what our partner is beneath their personality. At our core, everyone shines immaculately.

6. Be Quiet Occasionally—There is a spiritual saying from the East that when the mind is quiet the heart speaks. Actually the heart sings! When we turn within—become meditative—and the mind gets quiet, we begin to see the perfection in our lives and relationships. We begin to see that the apparent hindrances and obstacles on our journeys are really opportunities and teachers in disguise. There is a merciful force helping us to unfold our love. It is what Hindus call the *Satguru*, the inner Teacher. When the mind stops chattering, guilt, fear, hatred and anger dissolve into a sense that everything is as it needs to be. There is a plan, most of which is unknown by the conscious mind. It is from this knowingness that true compassion arises.

In your silent meditation, gently place the attention on the center of your chest. Each time your attention wanders away, notice the shift and gently bring it back.

7. Forgive Each Other—Forgiveness comes as we become receptive to the Beloved. From the heart we see that things happen as they must. Even a painful mistake, seen from the deeper spiritual perspective, is not really a mistake; it is just life unfolding. From the perspective of the heart, and the Beloved, there is nobody to blame. Everything is essentially perfect, so there is nothing to forgive.

From the personal perspective, however, forgiveness does serve a role. Forgiveness—as a spiritual practice—can cause us to investigate the roots of our reactive patterns. When an unskillful action on our part hurts another being, the need to forgive ourselves gives an inward push to our awareness. We are often forced to look below the surface to an underlying wound that might have caused our behavior. Forgiveness is a natural step in letting go.

The mind can also be pushed inward when somebody else's behavior hurts us, especially when we are unable to let go of our blame or resentment. This blame or resentment is tension inside us. And the longer we carry it around, the more damage we will incur. The practice of forgiveness causes us to ponder the roots of our suffering. It always has to do with separation in some way. As we are able to offer ourselves understanding of our own suffering, we find we are also able to extend it to others. The root of unskillful (unconscious) behavior is the same in all people: separation. When this is truly understood, forgiveness is a natural, automatic response.

When we move more completely into the heart, our awareness expands. Life continues to be expressed through us, but our awareness is no longer defined or identified by passing events. Conflicts arising from surface preferences and various quirks in the personality no longer bind us or occupy much time. Differences are celebrated like a garden of flowers, even when we are pricked by a thorn. Our love is not diminished.

MOVING FROM THE THIRD TO THE
FOURTH CHAKRA

The leap in alignment from the solar plexus, or third chakra, to the fourth chakra in the heart is a movement toward unconditional acceptance. This is the dawn of a less personal awareness. People in the West often find this concept of impersonal awareness difficult to understand because it calls into question our whole sense of ego identity. What do you mean I'm not my personality? Who am I if not my thoughts, feelings, and behavior patterns? This is a wonderful question that can only be answered in silence. Thus begins the sometimes shocking, sometimes painful transition into the very unconditional nature of the heart. The truth is that love is never experienced at the level of the personality. We have to move to our core, to our essence, to taste real love.

When Mother Teresa was asked how she could work so tirelessly with the poorest of the poor and the sick and dying, she replied that she was only serving Jesus in his various disguises. This is a perfect description of living fully from the heart. She was identified with God. She was not identified with the mind/body of the leper, but the perfect, immaculate Christ within. It was easy and joyful for Mother Teresa to serve the poor, because she saw the Beloved where others saw only filth and rags. She was literally caring for God.

We lose our desire to be involved in conflict when we understand that there is nobody to get angry at. From the fourth chakra, we experience each other in terms of the Beloved. Conflicts can still arise, anger can sometimes be expressed, and fear can still be experienced, but not for long. The intuitive understanding that everything is actually the Beloved in disguise quickly cuts off any involvement of the ego. Issues that used to be perceived in a very personal way are now merely witnessed. Love, simple acceptance of what is, is one's natural way of being, as we make the perceptual shift from personal attachments at the third chakra to the free and unconditional awareness of the heart.

As our perceptual framework shifts to unconditional acceptance, we see that conventional marriage up to this point was primarily founded on fear and insecurity. We owned and possessed each other like objects. Our happiness or sorrow was based upon the relative well-being of our partners and the ability to meet each other's physical and emotional needs. Nothing wrong here, but somewhere inside we inevitably live with the root chakra fear of loss. From this sense of personal attachment and corresponding fear of loss, arise all the various control issues that plague most couples. Jealousy, the obsessive need for attention, pleasing, begging, learned helplessness, the persecutor/victim game, the need to be a good lover—a list that goes on seemingly forever—arise out of a basic insecurity of the ego. It never occurs to us, until this transition into the heart is well begun, that the reason an individual like Mother Teresa ceased to suffer (though she was not immune to pain) is that she was less identified with her ego and all the myriad problems that arise from it. She married the Beloved. Most of us are not destined to be saints. But couples who cross the bridge into the pure heartland of the fourth chakra together experience a deep, unshakable peace and acceptance of life and one another. We live with an awareness of being both separate and one.

In the heart, there is no room for conflict, hatred, and blame. All such reactions cease when we stop identifying with the social conditioning surrounding personal power and control. Love at its root is free and unconditional. But peace is pure fancy so long as the mind, with its endless lists of wants and needs, is running the show. The ego—the mechanism of separateness—must go in order for love to blossom. The heart is the arena for this wondrous event.

ALIGNING OUR FIFTH CHAKRAS: CREATIVITY AND COMMUNICATION

The fifth chakra is centered at the throat and is the source of creativity, communication, joy, and sadness. It is closely connected to the second and third chakras of sex and emotional feeling as well.

Suppression of feeling is intimately linked to the shutting down of the throat chakra. As children, being taught such lessons as "Big kids don't cry" may have forced us to suppress our feelings. Now, as adults, many of us find that with sadness or grief comes an automatic tightening of our throat muscles. This is due to such childhood conditioning.

As we open the throat chakra, we discover a deep capacity for both feeling and expression. We allow for the full range of emotions—sadness, fear, anger, joy, praise, and gratitude. We learn to be simple and authentic in our communication. When the two of us first came together, the attraction was so potent that we spent days, weeks, and months sharing our personal journeys. It felt like a lock had been removed not only from our hearts but our mouths as well. Dreams, memories, and reflections came up that had never before been addressed or shared. This was the opening of our fifth chakras.

The passion of being together—though it naturally changes with time—will keep burning as long as we remain simple and clear with each other. Alignment of our fifth chakras means that we keep no vital secrets from each other and that we don't share intimate aspects of ourselves with others that we are not willing to share with each other.

The throat chakra is directly linked to our sexual centers. If we keep the lines of communication open, our sexual energies will remain strong. Often when couples complain of losing their sexual passion, it is actually caused by the withholding of important feelings or thoughts. In such instances, partners need more heartfelt dialogue in order to express what's on their minds and in their hearts. When we are able to identify what needs to be expressed, and then share it with our partner in a way that can be received, it's like turning on a light-switch. The magic starts flowing again and passion returns. What we are actually doing is turning on the psychic switch of our fifth chakras.

Here's an interesting story about such sharing. We worked with a couple who had been married about fifteen years. Each time we sat with them, we had this sense that something essential was not being shared. There was a clear desire on their parts to heal, but an emotional aridness pervaded their relationship. Finally we asked them to join a couples group that we led, and we decided to implement an exercise in deep sharing. We asked each couple to sit by a fire for a full twenty-four hours together and share any secrets that might be preventing their hearts from opening. We would meet again the following week in group to discuss their experiences.

As you can imagine, there was plenty of material to explore the following week! Nearly every couple was withholding something that was vital for their communication to deepen. Once the secrets were shared, these relationships opened to a whole new level of aliveness and intimacy. The couple that had previously felt so distant was now responding with great intensity toward each other. They were not exactly at peace, but they were certainly connecting emotionally and physically in a richer way. What was the bit of information they had finally communicated, which allowed their passion to reemerge?

It turned out that during the first few years of their relationship both had had other sexual partners. Out of shame, embarrassment and fear of losing their relationship, they finally put an end to the affairs, but they never dared share the truth with each other, and thus they never released their guilt. Keeping such secrets from each other is like putting a lock on a door of the inner heart with a sign saying "Do Not Enter"!

It was enough, in the case of this couple, to gradually drain away all their deepest desires for each other.

Now that they had shared their secrets, the loving excitement between them increased dramatically. The night of their sharing they went through several layers of emotional numbness and pain as they opened their hearts again. They finished their twenty-four hour vigil by making love in front of the fireplace.

Many others in the group had similar experiences, with the same opening up of their sexual energies as the communication went deeper. The key to the release of all this passion lay in the unlocking of their fifth chakras and the sharing of secret stories that had been left untold in their hearts.

Does this mean that we have to share everything with each other? Each couple is unique and must carefully examine the matter for themselves. In a spiritual partnership, where a strong commitment to truth clearly exists, it is best not to keep secrets. In keeping the secret we often have to shut down a place in our hearts, and this can't help but affect our intimacy with each other.

Although, in general, we advocate for full disclosure, this doesn't mean we must share every detail of our lives; but it does mean that we are willing to—and to become increasingly transparent.

The fifth chakra is also a center for our creativity. When couples cease the games of avoidance and suppression, tremendous creative energies become available. It is at this point that couples get inspired to engage in various creative projects together—whether it is art, film, science, business, volunteer work, or whatever naturally interests them. Depending on the stage of one's life, the opening of the fifth chakra can create a desire for children as well.

Here are some pointers for opening and aligning our fifth chakras through communication.

1. Avoid Keeping Secrets from Each Other—Look upon truthfulness as a spiritual practice. Secrets keep the heart guarded. As we've mentioned before, in conventional relationships it might be too disruptive to share our deepest secrets, and thus the need to hold back. But in a spiritual partnership an enormous opportunity will be missed by keeping secrets. The heart will have to shut down to protect the secret information, and our partner will feel it intuitively.

It is important in strengthening our alignment with each other that we not share with others what we are not first willing to share with our partners. The emphasis is on the word willing. Such willingness to tell our partner everything helps us to stay conscious and united in our communication. In sharing with our partner in this way, we avoid telling casual friends about intimate aspects of our relationship that are more effectively processed with our partners. And this protects our relationship.

Perhaps you've had an experience with a friend who wants to know too much about your relationship with your partner. When we are frightened by the prospect of intimacy, our mind looks for a way out. When this is the case, it is not uncommon to attract individuals who, due their own negativity, support our own need to avoid intimacy. Such individuals often find meaning in becoming our confidantes, and we may find ourselves sharing intimate details of our relationship that really ought to be shared with our partners instead. We often leave such encounters feeling reinforced in our separateness, and as a result the alignment with our partners is weakened. It is better to share our concerns about our partnership with our partner first. Then, if we need outside support, we can find an appropriate source, a serious friend to both of us, or perhaps a qualified counselor, whose only agenda is to help in the resolution of our conflict.

2. Do Not Suppress Feelings That Want to Arise—For example, it's appropriate to share your anger with your partner as long as it doesn't last too long or reach the level of rage.

If you need to deal with heavy emotions like rage, going to a private place like a bedroom or basement and screaming into a pillow can be helpful. Imagine that your throat is opening up wide. Breathe deep into your belly and push out all the suppressed pain inside. Make as much sound as you absolutely can, growling, snarling, cursing—or whatever feels appropriate. When the desire to get your feelings out subsides, lay down with your eyes closed and gently bring your awareness to your throat chakra. Hold it there for a few minutes, feeling any sensations that might arise. Now allow your awareness to float up and down your whole body, holding it for a few moments in any area where a strong feeling might reside.

When the throat chakra starts opening, all manner of repressed feelings can surface. Remember all the times you were told—or you told yourself—to just "keep your mouth shut"? When the throat closes, we simultaneously shut down our feelings. There is a very intimate connection between the throat chakra and the lower chakras most powerfully connected with emotions. Of course the heart chakra is greatly affected as well. How can the heart stay open when we can't express ourselves naturally?

A spiritual partnership provides a powerful stage on which to access and release stored up memories and past experiences, as we often play roles for each other when we remember our old hurts. The throat chakra is a powerful player in this process. As we go increasingly deeper into our relationship, we uncover, with the aide of greater shakti, subtler levels of repressed feeling and emotion. We must continue to express ourselves as a way of releasing those prior imprints.

We can do so not only via verbal expression—either alone or with each other—but through artistic means as well. Writing, painting, sculpting, playing music, acting, and other pursuits all provide a way to express our feelings. Still, with issues that are important to the relationship, it is best to communicate directly, face to face, heart to heart.

Sometimes containing the emotions that want to surface can be effective in driving awareness deeper to the root of the feeling. For example, if something happens to stimulate a particular distressing emotion, we can bring our awareness to it internally. Rather than saying or acting out anything, we can close our eyes and invite into our consciousness any feelings that float by. Such a process can be very painful, since we might find ourselves touching some very hot wires internally. But we know we've reached bottom when a sense of relaxation and well-being returns. Then, if any thoughts or feelings need to be shared, we can do so from an emotionally open space. Dealing with emotions in this way, internally, can take time depending on the situation, the person, and the strength of the reactive pattern.

Similarly, it can be a very powerful experience to consciously not respond verbally when our partner says or does something that causes an emotional reaction in us. Lose the argument. Be wrong. Feel the shifting reactions internally as you refuse to give into your typical patterns of flight or fight. Engaging in this non-response process can yield tremendous insight into the power of our habitual reactions. It soon becomes evident just how strong some of our patterns can be. At the same time, refusing to respond to incidents that typically cause us to feel hot emotions can be useful in developing a calm center.

3. Sing and Chant Together—Singing and chanting are some of the most enjoyable vehicles for opening the fifth chakras. For us, singing devotional songs is a regular spiritual practice at our home. No matter how fatigued we might be from our workday, after chanting awhile in the evening we feel wonderfully refreshed. Singing and chanting are also beneficial for releasing negative emotions.

4. Praise and Have Gratitude for All That the Beloved Has Brought Us—Couples who are on a conscious path must be careful not to overdo the processing of negativity. We can become too critical of ourselves and each other, and we must remember that we are not together just to process our difficulties. We are together to enjoy and explore life. Praise is the joyous language of the heart. Nothing opens the chakras more powerfully than using our voices to honestly praise life.

5. Be Silent Occasionally—Again, silence allows for our minds to become quiet so that we can be more aware of our inner life. Doors can open within that were closed at some point in our past. Silence heals—and is a way of resting our whole selves.

A question arises: How can there be anything left to purify or awaken once we are aligned in the fourth chakra of the heart? The chakras do not open in a perfectly sequential way, as this process of unification with the Beloved is not as linear as it sounds. Each chakra is part of a whole system, and their opening and closing affect each other. As our sexual chakra heals, all the different chakras are affected positively. As the throat gives voice to what is, the heart naturally relaxes—as do the other chakras. Each one interfaces with the others. Although we might refer to the sequential unfolding of the chakras, it is not a straight ahead process, especially in the context of relationship.

ALIGNING OUR SIXTH CHAKRAS: SPIRITUAL

Located between the eyebrows, this center is the basis of spiritual vision. When the third eye opens we appreciate each other in terms of the Beloved. Marriage becomes an act of worship. Lovemaking becomes a fire ceremony to the Divine. Preparing food for our mate becomes an offering to God. Service to one another becomes a way of showing gratitude to our Source.

When the sixth chakra is closed it can sometimes be the storehouse of anger. People with headaches originating in the forehead are often holding onto some frustration or anger. Have you ever noticed how we often furrow our brows when we are angry? We literally squeeze shut our higher spiritual perception of the situation.

As our spiritual vision opens, we experience increasing states of deep peace and calm. We see life as it is: a dance of incomprehensible mystery, the Beloved embodied in billions of different forms. Creation is unfolding with a perfection the mind cannot grasp. The thumb print of the Beloved is on every blade of grass, on every strand of hair, in every single event. Nothing can happen that is not ordained by the Universe. The Divine is present in every moment.

Here is a powerful exercise for aligning spiritual vision:

Build a warm fire (If you do not have a fireplace, light some candles). Now facing each other close your eyes and bring your attention up to the third eye, the space between the eyebrows. After two or three minutes, visualize a radiant indigo beam of light connecting you at this point. Let yourself feel the warm, pulsating light of your chakras flowing between you. Take a few deep breaths and give thanks internally for your spiritual partnership and the opportunity to make the journey together. Now simply keep your attention at the point between your eyebrows. Each time attention wanders, bring it back to this point. After about twenty minutes, open your eyes and enjoy. Do this simple meditation every day together. (You don't need to build a fire each time.)

ALIGNING OUR SEVENTH CHAKRAS: TRANSCENDENCE

The seventh chakra corresponds to transcendence. This chakra has no shadow, no polarity of experience associated with it. It is the experience of total liberation and union with God. It is the awareness of complete wholeness, the transcendence of all duality, unity consciousness. The American Indian headdress is symbolic of an awakened seventh chakra, as is a gold crown. Bonding at the seventh chakra is about the choiceless surrender to God. For a relationship to support us spiritually—in the highest sense of the word—God, the One—must become the central issue, the spiritual still-point behind all forms of relating. It is from here, at the still-point, that everything else finds balance and toward which everything else in our lives is guided. Like a triad we are each joined by God at the apex, or crown. We must each turn to our spiritual core, not our ego, when deep nourishment and understanding are required.

Form does not sustain or nurture life; Spirit sustains and nurtures form. We need only watch someone die to grasp the significance of this truth. One moment the body is pulsating, alive and beautiful, the next it is completely still. When the Spirit departs, the body is finished. The element of beauty, of attraction, was not the body, but the Spirit within it. Likewise, it is the spiritual essence, or Beloved, that gives vitality, well-being and balance to our relationship. Our relationship to each other is but a symbolic gesture, a fleeting shadow of the dance we do eternally with our Beloved. This is the heavy symbology behind the wedding ceremony. It is a representation of the alchemical invisible inner wedding, the true marriage of the individual to the Beloved, the form to the formless.

It is our attachment to form and its inherently fickle nature that causes our suffering.

In times of conflict we reference ourselves to each other, to the body of the relationship, rather than to the Spirit behind it. Rather than the relationship pointing us to the Beloved, we look to each other. *The Course In Miracles* calls this type of relationship special in that we deny the true source of love and turn our partners into idols. We live with a chronic, often unconscious fear of loss. Such attachment to form reinforces a subtle sense of separateness between us, which, as we have seen, becomes the basis for the arising of all manner of shadow emotions such as anger, jealousy, fear, hatred and guilt. Any time we are stuck in conflict we are looking to the ego for support. We have lost sight of the pure spirit of truth that dwells beyond the mind.

Healing takes place when we uncompromisingly turn our intention inward to the apex, the Beloved. It is at this moment that we become receptive.

Once we truly open up we see our interconnectedness, and most importantly, where we interconnect. Some simple questions or koans to help us get free at this level are: What is the highest truth at this moment? Who or what is in control here? What do I refuse to accept in the present moment?

In pondering deeply any of these koans, our awareness will gradually come to rest again in the heart, with the Beloved. Conflict is always based on a sense of separation and is thus rooted in the ego. As we free our attention from the apparent external cause of our pain—for example, something in our relationship—the truth of our inherent relatedness reemerges. We meet again in the sacred, open space within, where there is no other and thus no conflict. There is only the Beloved. It is from this basis that we teach the necessity of placing the truth of our oneness at the heart of the relationship.

At the crown chakra the primary purpose of our relationship is the enjoyment of unity. Here we play in the fields of the Lord. Here we meet together in Spirit without much sense of other in the heart. The surrendering of duality, the sacrifice of the ego, and the birth into union are the highest gifts of a spiritual partnership. Our surrender is not actually to one another but to that unified Presence which the relationship represents.

A question often arises: Do we need to worship the same form of God? Not always. The most important factor is that we each recognize the need for the transcendent in whatever form it comes. We have met couples who are both deeply devoted to God, yet one shares a stronger affinity for one form over that of the other. Two of our dearest friends are both devoted Christians, yet one is also an American Indian who holds in her heart more space for other expressions of God. These two people are deeply aligned spiritually. Their devotion to each other and to God is as powerful as that of anyone we've met. Yet they have an added spiritual dimension, and it works beautifully for them.

Generally, it is helpful when partners walk the same path, so that the same spiritual values and instructions infuse both hearts and the daily lives of both people. But there are no absolutes. It is more important to respect each other's paths than to walk the same one.

The yoga of relationship is the subtle, exquisite alignment of each aspect of our being. How we sexually embrace, fight, breathe, live, die, and rebirth together, all are different postures (asanas) in this teaching. Sometimes we imitate the bull, trying to push our way through conflict at first. But finally we learn how to endure and be patient. Or suddenly a sharp comment pricks our pride, and we roar like a lion. At other times, defending ourselves, we spit like a cobra. But as we learn to hold the pose and awareness penetrates deep into the heart of each movement, we discover a certain unalloyed joy and confidence at our core. We become inwardly quiet, open, flexible, and strong. We are whole—even as we break—and in our wholeness we find a profound capacity to embrace others in their wholeness, even as they break.

Yoga means singular, one-pointed. To love one other person fully, to align and remain aligned at each spiritual center, is to awaken a big Love for all.

When the one man loves the one woman,
And the one woman loves the one man,
The very angels desert heaven
And come and sit in that house and sing for joy.
—Brahma Sutra

CHAPTER EIGHT

Sexual Communion

*A thousand half-loves must
be forsaken to take one
whole heart home.*
—RUMI

It was a chilly, late summer evening in the high Cascades of Oregon. A bright full moon crept up over the rocky crags of the east crater wall. Aside from the occasional splash of a rainbow trout, the lake was completely still; but not so for us. We hugged and kissed in our new brown sleeping bags with all the intensity of young lovers. Suddenly, Faye pulled back and said, "Honey, if we keep on this way we're going to have us a baby!" We eased up momentarily.

Five minutes passed, when a whole new surge of energy kicked in. Shakti streamed throughout our bodies, transforming physical pleasure into deep spiritual joy and bliss.

Twenty-two years later I still have a mental picture of the moon's reflection in Faye's big green eyes. There is still within me a pool of ecstasy from which our first child, Julian, was conceived on that auspicious eve in the high mountains. At that time, we knew very little about sacred sex from a technical point of view. But experientially we realized that sex— under conscious loving conditions—could become a powerful vehicle for ecstatic spiritual sharing. We found that sexual energy both pleasured and healed us.

In this chapter we are going to explore sexual expression as a way of spiritual communion in the heart. We will share an understanding that will allow us to experience not only much greater pleasure but deeper intimacy with each other and the Beloved.

Sex is deeply misunderstood in virtually every civilized culture. Social and religious conditioning based on the fear of original sin (a patriarchal doctrine, which conveys that we are separate from the Divine) has done much to block the hidden secrets of conscious lovemaking. Reinforcing this conditioning is our sense of not feeling loved, which develops at some point in childhood as our separate egos take shape. As a result, the connection to our life-energy, or shakti, is weakened, and our minds become tense. As we enter adulthood, sex becomes one way of superficially releasing the build up of this primal tension, or knot, in the psyche. It becomes a kind of control mechanism and release valve for our stressed egos. From a conventional perspective the focus of sex is on orgasm and release. At that moment, however briefly, the tension of the ego is discharged and our whole system relaxes. It is like having a good sneeze.

In sexual communion, we open more deeply. Our focus shifts from having orgasm to opening into the heart. We expand and extend physical pleasure until the mind, or ego, is released. It is here—in the heart—that the deepest internal knots are dissolved and a profound sense of well-being flowers. In deep lovemaking the heart is undressed and we unite with our deepest spiritual essence.

Why, then, is there confusion in many spiritual schools about sex? Much of it has to do with fear. For several thousand years spiritual teachings have been dominated by patriarchy, the split between mind and body, and a hierarchy in which the mind is viewed as far superior to and more holy than the body. The mind, or masculine principle, unconsciously fears the natural instincts of the body, the feminine principle, because when fully engaged sexually, it loses control; our attention is literally booted out of our heads and returns to our hearts. Thus, spiritual traditions evolved which emphasized the renunciation of the body—and its delightfully sexual nature—as a way of liberation. Such approaches do work for special individuals. But often they are used unknowingly as subconscious strategies of the mind for maintaining its sense of separateness, domination and control. Our relationship to the world—and to one another—is a reflection of our subtle relationship to our bodies.

On the other hand, sex without love can be dangerous and damaging to life. It can be used for control, manipulation and ego-gratification. And because of its immense power over the rational mind, individuals can become addicted to the release. Thus, many spiritual paths offer caution to their students in working with their sexual energies. There is wisdom here. But for spiritual seekers whose hearts are cultivated and who find themselves in a loving relationship, sex becomes an exquisite doorway into the Spirit.

Conscious sex dissolves the separation between mind and body, head and heart, masculine and feminine. It floods the cells of our bodies with joy. In deep sexual communion our entire consciousness gets reoriented toward the care and protection of life. As the heart opens through sexual love we spontaneously seek a cooperative relationship with each other and the world. It is a form of Holy Communion wherein we consume the body as sacrament and through patience and care enter the sanctum sanctorum of the Heart.

THE DANCE OF SEXUAL COMMUNION AND THE HARMONY OF GOOD SEX

The world is pervaded by shakti. Everything is created, maintained, and destroyed by the power of shakti. Shakti is one with sexual energy. Nowhere is the dance of shakti more clearly manifested than in the sexual act. Our consciousness lights up in sex. Because of the dramatic intensification of shakti in lovemaking, an opportunity is present for transcendent experience. The key lies in bringing deep, loving awareness to our sexuality and for the male to become skillful in the postponement of ejaculation.

When ejaculation in the male is delayed, the shakti that is generated and normally released quickly through the genitals can be easily directed upward into the higher centers and allowed to flow throughout the entire body for deep rejuvenation and healing. This is the true art of lovemaking. Rather than the sexual act taking a matter of minutes, the climax can be delayed and pleasure dramatically intensified for virtually hours. When we bring awareness into the sexual dance, we enliven a powerfully harmonizing energy between us.

The entire universe is composed of positive and negative, masculine and feminine, yang and yin forces. All of life is an exquisite and sensual dance of opposites from subatomic particles to huge galaxies spanning light years. As Jungian psychology has informed us, each person, regardless of gender, has within him both masculine (yang) as well as feminine (yin) qualities. The path of coming into wholeness, or individuation as Jung referred to it, is an alchemical process of harmonizing these two opposing forces. Nowhere is this process more evident than in the sportive, erotic, dance of intimacy. Because these forces are psychic as well as physical, these teachings apply to many same sex relationships.

When a man and woman truly commune sexually—bringing loving care and awareness into the act—the natural polarities come into balance. Man becomes more attuned to his receptive feminine side. Woman becomes more attuned to her focused masculine side. This allows for integration within whereby the interconnected opposites begin coexisting harmoniously. The psychic knot of duality (separateness) and the mental tension it generates not only get discharged but are provided a way to heal. In Tantra, this process of integration is called the marriage of Shiva and Shakti.

It's important to acknowledge that in integrating our feminine and masculine energies, we by no means lose any aspect of our essential gender specific qualities. It is a spiritual law that opposites ultimately strengthen one another. As men and women become more attuned to each other during sexual communion, it has a strengthening effect on their essential gender qualities. After full sexual intercourse a man feels more alive and energized in his basic maleness, and a woman feels fuller and more powerful in her receptive femininity. Both experience a revitalization of their wholeness.

A word of caution: couples are ready for sexual communion only when they have attained a certain level of emotional responsibility, psychological awareness, and a strong love of the Divine. And, of course, they must love each other. Without love for each other and the Divine, and without a sense of emotional responsibility and psychological awareness, sex is simply a disguised form of self-pleasuring and tension release. Instead of circulating gold, couples exchange the mud of latent guilt and resentment.

In previous chapters we have discussed various types of conflict within a relationship, many of which are centered on betrayal, anger, or fear. At its root, all conflict is the result of a build-up of tension and fear caused by the feeling of separation from our source, from the Beloved. The mind—or ego— is the instrument responsible for this illusion. Wanting relief from tension, the mind fights mercilessly to maintain the illusion of its separate existence. The mind's struggle for self-preservation is simply another name for conflict. The mind resists love and experiences pain in surrender. In deep sexual communion, our basic duality is transcended, masculine/feminine energies are harmonized, and the essential cause of conflict and suffering dissipates.

In the dance of sexual communion, as men we learn to go slow and relax fully into the experience, we allow the energy to build up and circulate throughout our systems. For women, as our men bring more presence and patience into the bedroom, we are able to have multiple orgasms and effortlessly circulate the healing energy throughout our entire bodies. The endocrine system, when sexually stimulated, produces wonderfully rejuvenating chemicals which flood our internal organs. In this process whatever imbalances exist physically, emotionally, or psychologically, tend to surface and get released. Remember, sexual energy is life energy. Life energy always seeks restoration of balance and well-being.

Beyond the biological effects of sexual communion, as we learn to surrender more fully into the entire experience and as we open fully to one another, a powerful psychological integration is cultivated. For example, what might be the effect of sexual communion on a couple whose polarity is reversed? That is, where the woman's masculine side is over-developed, resulting in her being too aggressive, and the man's feminine side is over-developed, resulting in his being too passive? Such imbalances are, at least partly, childhood adaptations caused by trauma, and these wounds are stored in our physical and emotional bodies.

In sexual communion, a woman who learns to fully receive her male partner finally feels safe expressing her femininity. And a man who learns to fully embrace his female partner finally finds safety in expressing his strong masculine side in a way that simultaneously supports and nurtures his relationship.

In sexual communion we are activating and drawing on the most powerful healing forces in the universe. It is the Kundalini shakti tapped by the yogis in the Himalayas and around the world. It is the chi cultivated in the martial arts and sacred Taoist practices of China and Southeast Asia. It is the Holy Spirit of the Christian Charismatic. It is the same power that manifests a mighty oak tree and that spins planets around a central sun. Our sexual energy is the primal source of all life, of all healing. Through sexual communion, we are reconnected to a deep sense of wholeness, which had been severed in childhood during the formation of our egos. All the chakras get awakened in deep lovemaking.

Through this reconnection, extremes in our psychology are subtly balanced. Macho men in surrendering fully to their partners learn to trust their feminine and find a greater capacity to nurture. Overly passive women, in learning to open to their male partners, find greater clarity in decision-making and action. Both learn to trust the opposite energy represented in one another. This life-energy or shakti works with our natural predilections so that the process of transformation is subtle and natural—like the growth of a flower or tree.

Shakti is represented symbolically in the ancient Caduceus, the emblem of the American Medical Association. The Caduceus is an alchemical symbol for the primal Shakti stored at the base of the spine—the first (earth) chakra, which is awakened during healing. Two snakes (phallic symbols) wind there way up the staff of life, representing the masculine/feminine energies winding their way up the spinal column and merging in the head at the crown chakra. As the shakti climbs the spinal column it merges at the third eye (sky) chakra, symbolizing wholeness, or the Invisible Wedding. The same healing force symbolized in the Caduceus is awakened during deep sexual communion. Our systems take from this healing force whatever is needed to restore physical, emotional and spiritual balance. As sex becomes life-affirming, rejuvenating, and harmonizing, men and women who surrender to the path of sexual communion find a heightening of physical well-being and self-awareness.

We are cosmic creatures—intimate, open, and inclined to share ourselves with each other. And we have within our bodies a cornucopia of precious substances and chemicals capable of creating, harmonizing and transforming life at all levels. Like the two of us, couples who experience the sense of wholeness in sexual communion find that their discovery is tantamount to finding the Holy Grail.

PRESENCE

For most people, a strong commitment to each other helps create the safety needed to open fully into the healing experience of intimacy The more faith we have in our partners the deeper our surrender. In the cultivation of this kind of intimacy many old wounds can arise, especially when there is a history of abandonment, sexual betrayal or abuse. Paradoxically, love brings up everything unlike itself.

To be truly naked and exposed to our partners is a form of confession. This process of intimate confession, whether it arises before, during, or after lovemaking, must be respected and cherished by both partners. Secrets are often shared between intimate partners, and both need to know how to listen to and take in such information. For example, partners might tell each other: I have an emotional handicap. I was violated when I was ten years old by my grandfather. I was betrayed at sixteen by my first girlfriend. I abandoned a lover. I violated a friend. In a loving relationship, sexual energy purifies and frees us from our inhibitions and subconscious fears. As we let go of guilt and old conditioning, we begin to radiate from a deeper stratum of our being and are not only able to share secrets with our partner but to bring a strong, safe presence into the relationship so that we can hear what they want to tell us.

Confession is not always verbal. We are simply referring to a deeper level of self-disclosure and a willingness to be vulnerable with our partners. A loving, committed relationship provides fertile soil for this kind of soul growth.

But there is an even deeper commitment than the one to our partner: our commitment to the Divine. It is our connection to Spirit that infuses our relationship with the capacity to open fully to one another. It is our surrender to God that allows us to be truly present for each other. Otherwise, our commitment will invariably come with hidden conditions of the mind. I'll love you if . . . I'll love you as long as you . . . But the heart that knows God is open, unrestrained in the moment, and capable of loving without conditions. Such a heart embodies real presence. It is the depth of our presence, based on the silence within, that allows us to surrender into the mystery of sex—and life—together.

EGO TRANSCENDENCE

When, through prolonged sexual sharing, our attention is directed upward into the higher centers of the body, our lust and urge toward self-gratification get sacrificed into the fires of devotional love. We joyously merge with one another. We are ecstatically and radiantly fused. Egos dissolve and a genuine sense of unity and bliss pervade our entire being. This is divine communion. The heat and passion of our sexuality consume our habitual mode of self-preoccupation.

The key to this kind of lovemaking lies with the quality of heart we bring to it and in gently directing the energies upward, instead of out through the discharging of semen. Women do not have to be as concerned here as men, as they do not lose much energy from orgasm. But their power of attention still must be activated to allow the energy to move beyond mere genital stimulation. During sexual communion, when our genitals become stimulated, we want to draw the energy up into the higher centers through the power of our attention and breath. The pleasure from our lower chakras is thus transmuted into bliss at the higher levels of the heart, third eye, and crown. Very little effort is needed to bring this about—in fact, the less the better. One way is to simply relax our breathing just prior to orgasm and bring our attention up to the heart or to the point between the eyebrows.

DELAYING THE MALE ORGASM

Delaying the orgasm is really a very practical consideration. We have referred a number of times to the importance of delaying male orgasm, but we must be careful not to get into a negative or guilty frame of mind in this regard. And we don't want to become preoccupied with it either.

The primary benefits include:

1. Greater Pleasure—Delaying orgasm allows for amplified pleasure, both in terms of intensity and longevity. It pleasures not only the male partner but the female partner as well.

It is a biological fact that men approach climax much more quickly than women. This is one important difference between masculine (yang) and feminine (yin) energies. Yang energy heats up more rapidly. Yin energy heats up much more gradually and needs more foreplay to bring itself to fulfillment. Thus, as males learn to postpone their orgasms, they allow their female partners the opportunity of much longer and deeper orgasms and therefore more pleasure. Delaying their own orgasm thus becomes a precious opportunity to give back to their partners.

2. Rejuvenated Sexual Energy—Learning to delay orgasm allows men to circulate the life-giving properties of their sexual chemistry beyond their genitals out to the rest of their bodies and vital organs. This results in tremendous rejuvenation during and after lovemaking, as opposed to the typical male feeling of being somewhat drained afterward. The art of conscious lovemaking has tremendous health benefits that have yet to be adequately researched by modern science.

3. Revitalized Higher Chakras—When men delay orgasm they have the opportunity to direct their sexual energy up into the higher chakras for a transcendent experience with their partners. In this way, they heal not only physically but psychologically and spiritually as well.

Beyond physical pleasure there is a joy that we experience in the heart together as we let go deeper into our sexual play. We meet beyond our personas, in the inner sanctum of the Heart.

So how do men go about delaying orgasm? The first step is to relax. As you approach orgasm breathe slowly and relax. Feel the energy flowing throughout your body. Feel it in your chest, arms, hands and fingers, legs, and moving up your back. Stay quiet. Don't move. Pay special attention at first to relaxing your pelvis and your thighs. Freedom of tension in these areas allows you to enjoy longer without climaxing. As the crisis of orgasm subsides, slowly begin whatever movements naturally arise. And pay close attention to your partner's rhythm. She will naturally take longer to warm up, and by tuning into her rhythm you will naturally tend to go slower as well.

For women, learn to be attentive to the rhythm of your partner. Tune into his passion, even as you open to your own. As you feel him approaching an early climax, relax with him. As the process continues and his capacity to sustain sexual arousal grows, you will naturally develop the faith to let go deeper into your own experience. Obviously, you do not need to be concerned about retaining your sexual juices. Your resources are practically infinite! But learning to attune to your partner will help both of you fulfill your sexual potential. As you go deeper into the sexual experience the heart will begin to open, and you will feel as if you are being embraced by the Beloved.

Each time the energy builds and subsides you will find that the next arousal is more intense and more enduring. You will, after several cycles, find that you can remain passionate for much longer periods of time. As the chakras open through deep embrace you will experience a high level of attunement.

Also experiment with little or no movement. Simply be with each other for one or two hours with little or no movement. Maintain just enough play to stay aroused but nothing more. Breathe together, maintaining as much eye contact as you can. Such connectedness is deeply healing and balancing.

If possible, do not bring any guilt or performance into your lovemaking. Keep it natural and loose. Working consciously with our sexual energy allows us to go much more deeply into the whole sexual terrain and beyond the physical body into the joyful, unified realm of the heart. We tap tremendous amounts of energy the deeper we dive.

What matters most in the dance of sexual communion is the quality of awareness that we bring to the experience. In lovemaking our subconscious energies are awakened because sex is like a mirror. We connect with deeper places within. It takes a refined, meditative awareness and a willing heart to fully appreciate all the subtle nuances of this delicate art. Dualistic concepts of internal/external, mind/body, male/female, and right/wrong fade away at the peak of transcendental love. As William Blake proclaimed: *Energy Is Eternal Delight.*

David says: Making love with Faye has taught me more about the human psyche than a decade of academic study in psychology. It has taught me more about the human spirit than thirty-five years of daily meditation practice. She has whispered the most esoteric secrets of all to me: *The best teacher is always Love. All questions are answered in love.*

SEXUAL COMMUNION PRINCIPLES

Below are thirteen essential principles on sexual communion. (For readers already in a partnership, try reading them aloud to each other.)

1. In Spiritual Partnerships We Recognize the Sanctity of the Physical World as the Foundation for Spiritual Opening—We do not evolve spiritually by denying our physical natures. On the contrary, desire can be a doorway to our divinity. Our sexual energy is the sacred fire that compels the human spirit toward greater bliss, finally culminating in the bliss of spiritual union.

There is sacrifice in love. Sacrifice has a negative connotation in the West and is often associated with suffering and denial. But in older traditions sacrifice is simply the idea of death and rebirth. We let go of the old to ring in the new. We transcend the ego to reawaken the wholeness of love. The oldest form of ritual depicting this great truth is the fire ceremony. Ancient traditional societies teach that fire is the mouth of God. It is believed whatever we offer with love to the fire goes straight to the Divine.

For the last ten years on our farm in Oregon we have started and ended the day with a simple fire ceremony called *Agnihotra*—offering back to God a little rice and clarified butter for all that we receive. With the chanting of mantras we acknowledge that everything belongs to God. Nothing belongs to us, not even our egos. When a man and woman offer their primal essence to each other, they are also reenacting an ancient fire ceremony. The ego lets go, love and devotion infuse their sexual juices, and Nature rejoices in the rejoicing of lovers.

2. In the Sacred Dance of Lovemaking Man and Woman Come Into Deeper Attunement with the Forces of Natural Law— Sexual communion is a perfect form of divine worship in that we view our partner as a manifestation of Spirit. And our coming together signifies the fusion of natural forces. All things in the universe are conceived through the harmonious fusion of positive and negative forces. In this cosmic play, man becomes a conduit for the positive forces (yang) and woman becomes a conduit for the negative forces (yin).

When yang and yin forces come together under the umbrella of sacred sexual communion, a fire sacrifice of individual egos is made. Both partners experience a state of greater bliss and balance, and the social environment subtly benefits. The laws of nature celebrate this marriage of heaven and earth, of masculine and feminine—this Invisible Wedding—and the couple naturally enjoys greater happiness in life.

In ancient societies, kings and queens and Tantric adepts would engage in elaborate sexual rituals as a way of balancing the forces of Nature, which in turn would benefit the kingdom with adequate rain, good crops, and general prosperity. Today such practices would no doubt be approached with enormous skepticism. But people in previous times were more meditative, their minds were less cluttered, and they were thus more sensitive to the subtle workings of Nature. Older cultures understand the science and art of ceremony—and the wisdom hidden therein.

3. Sexual Communion is an Intuitive Art That is Best Learned with Minimum Instruction—Bringing one's awareness into the sexual act is often enough. From here everything we need to know simply gets revealed. It all comes naturally, without effort. Being deeply present for one another is love-making, whether intercourse happens or not.

4. A Loving Attitude is More Important than the Technique— A loving attitude is not a moral or intellectual consideration. It has to do with bringing a sense of reverence for our partners into the sexual moment.

A loving attitude is simply the natural disposition of hearts unfettered by unconscious guilt, resentment and fear. Reverence for one another arises spontaneously as deeper levels of heart are explored together and shadows are shared and integrated. As we truly fall in love with the Divine our hearts become open, innocent, and caring.

5. Spontaneity Always Takes Precedence Over Strategy— The body knows exactly what to do when the mind has no agenda for it. Gently ponder the sexual secrets; then forget about it. Let the conditioning change naturally, without effort.

6. Meditative Awareness is a Fundamental Key to Sexual Communion—Meditative awareness automatically takes into account intuition, right attitude, and spontaneity. Meditative awareness is simple, uncluttered, relaxed, innocent, and open. We don't push. We don't manipulate. We don't try. We don't force. We don't rush. If you find yourself reverting back to being goal-oriented, simply shift into relaxing without judgment. In meditative awareness we just open to what is.

Our bodies do not need coaching to get turned on. Our bodies benefit from the mind's nonjudgmental acceptance of passion, flow, and desire. Meditative awareness is simply cooperating with what is happening in the moment. No judgments. No agendas. No ambition. In meditative awareness everything is perfect as it is, so nothing needs to be fixed or controlled. We don't need to milk every drop of pleasure from our bodies like a hungry infant. It is okay to ejaculate, or not.

Should tension arise, remember to relax. Bring your attention to the place in the body that is holding tension. Breathe into it for a few minutes. Gently resist the temptation to release the tension through conventional orgasm.

Go slowly. Take plenty of time. As the male moves toward orgasm, just relax and let go of the need. Take awhile to be completely still. Breathe into empty space. And when you feel calm, begin the dance of arousal again if you wish.

To make love this way is to play in the fields of the Lord. As the mind becomes quiet and meditative, the body becomes loose and supple.

7. Men Need to Control Orgasm and Harmonize with the Longer, Deeper Rhythms of the Female—By gently delaying the outer orgasm and at the same time letting go of control, both partners move into deeper levels of openness and well-being. Sexual communion teaches us that there is no hurry in love, no agenda to fulfill, just simplicity and innocence.

Achievement and control are masculine-oriented inclinations. To bring depth and healing to the sexual dance we must let go of such tendencies during lovemaking. The feminine has much to teach the world in this regard.

It is a great gift for a woman when a man waits until she is nice and juicy before entering her. Yin is by nature cooler than yang at first, thus a male lover needs to be more patient, giving her plenty of time to warm up. Also the left side of the body is more sensitive for a woman. When a man begins the dance of sexual communion by gently kissing and stroking the right side first, it gives his partner time to gently open. Then, as she warms up, the man can begin to caress and kiss her left side. It's good to wait twenty or thirty minutes before fully entering her.

This more conscious approach to lovemaking results in greater attunement and relaxation for both partners. When a woman is fully prepared and ready to receive her partner, both experience a deeper level of satisfaction. Passion is best sustained when built up slowly. It is equally important for a woman to stay attuned to her male partner. Follow your passion more slowly, and get to know the way of your lover.

Eventually a delightful secret is uncovered: men can orgasm internally without ejaculation of semen. It takes practice, sensitivity, and awareness, but over time men can find themselves riding strong internal waves of pleasure, rising and falling throughout their entire bodies, without any loss of semen. This is sometimes referred to as a valley orgasm. It's a profoundly healing experience; leaving men feeling physically refreshed and emotionally open.

Women instinctively know the subtle nuances of the sexual dance. When males can attune themselves to the slower cycle of the female, there is greater sexual fulfillment for both partners.

8. Awareness and Breath are the Essential King and Queen of Healing—By cultivating awareness and breath we can both deepen and extend our lovemaking almost indefinitely.

It is a simple natural law that energy follows awareness. In sexual communion we are churning the primal waters, the shakti which animates, enlivens, and fuels everything in creation. As the shakti builds up in our bodies we can experience this as a form of tension and want to immediately discharge it.

This is precisely what happens with conventional orgasm. We get turned on until we can no longer handle the tension (the energy) and we ejaculate. This is particularly true of men but also true of women who are unable to relax.

With the simple use of our awareness and our breath we can disperse the build up of energy to other parts of our bodies and thus transcend the chronic need to orgasm. For both sexes, just shy of orgasm, relax completely, breathe deeply, stop all movement and bring your attention from the genitals up to the heart. In doing this, you will begin to feel the pleasure extending to your chest. After a few minutes allow the attention to move up into the head and out into the arms, legs, and toes. Explore. Feel with attention your whole body. Continue the slow, deep breath. You will notice that your entire system is enjoying the currents of shakti generated by your lovemaking.

With simple awareness and breath we can enliven our whole mind/body with healing energy. The more we repeat this cycle the more energy builds and circulates throughout our systems. This is how sexual communion becomes rejuvenating rather than depleting as in conventional sex.

9. Women Play a Key Role in Supporting Men as They Learn the Art of Sexual Communion—A woman has the capacity to have multiple orgasms and to generate seemingly inexhaustible amounts of shakti through sexual communion. For this reason, she plays a key role in guiding her partner beyond the mind and its limited form of conventional orgasm.

As we attune ourselves to one another, we become sensitive to the natural rhythms of our dance together. A woman begins to sense when her partner is approaching orgasm. This is the time to relax, be gentle and allow her partner to channel his energy upward and toward her, rather than out. In tune with her partner, now is the time to bring her own attention into the higher chakras and to allow the shakti to circulate accordingly. Shakti follows attention. A woman does not need to withhold her own orgasm, only to be sensitive to where her partner is in the energy cycle. Both can share in the silence and stillness that come with this phase.

In this dance, couples quite naturally take turns giving and receiving energy. At times the male takes a more dominant position. At other times the female assumes it. Once the inclination toward orgasm is let go, the dance begins again. In this way, sexual communion can go on for hours, if we choose. Each new cycle brings more intensity and the ability to last longer before reaching orgasm. Each time we commune together at more ecstatic and intimate levels.

Be sure and play with different sexual positions. Man on top, or woman on top. Side positions. Man sitting cross-legged, with woman sitting on top with legs outstretched around her lover. Switching positions and giving and receiving at different times add spice and intensity to the dance. Do not suppress your voice if sounds wish to be expressed. Different sounds may arise naturally as the energy opens up in various ways in our bodies.

After we have repeated this energy cycle several times we may decide we want to orgasm in the conventional way. Most couples find that by this time the orgasm is dramatically more powerful. Give yourselves over to it completely. Go into it as deeply and fully as possible. Much healing energy has been generated and circulated in your bodies, and you will not generally feel drained after ejaculation. On the contrary most people feel revitalized and deeply relaxed.

10. The Purifying Power of Sexual Communion Enables Emotional Blockages to Surface for Healing—It is not uncommon to encounter occasional periods of emotional roughness following, or possibly even during, extended lovemaking. Profound levels of intimacy naturally challenge any tensions residing in the unconscious. Old hurts surrounding experiences of abandonment, betrayal, sexual and emotional abuse, religious guilt, and rejection can manifest with greater intensity than we might normally be accustomed to. Relax as much as possible. Feelings of vulnerability are natural. Be careful not to judge or push away from any experience—positive or negative—that arises during or after lovemaking. This is where psychological understanding can be very useful. Sexual communion, at the level we are discussing, can stir up deep knots and be very cathartic, especially for a day or two after the session.

Bringing a calm, focused presence to the reactive pattern as it arises will help to dismantle it; avoid judgment and feel its naked quality.

At the same time, breathing into any uncomfortable sensations that might be surfacing is also helpful. During lovemaking, we can also synchronize our breathing patterns and instruct our partners to mentally direct loving kindness to us. It's also very healing to share with each other any feelings of vulnerability that might be arising.

Lovemaking is natural. Let it be easy. Let it be joyful. When feelings of vulnerability arise either during or after intense lovemaking, affirm that the heart is in the process of opening yet more. See it not as an obstacle but as an opportunity for deeper understanding, for more compassion, for more letting go. The fire of love is consuming the pain.

11. Sexual Communion is a Doorway to the Ecstatic Nature of the Self—the Target is God, Not Sex—The real secret behind our sexual play is that at the deepest level we are bonding with the Beloved. Joy does not originate outside ourselves nor does it reside in the apparent object of our desire, our partner. Joy is a quality of the Self and a gift of the Beloved.

The scriptures tell us that the nature of the Self is blissful, conscious, and eternally stable. All desire arising from the mind and body, no matter what form it takes, is fundamentally homesickness, a deep yearning to get back to the Beloved—to the joyful, peaceful nature of the Self. Many people obsess over sex because unconsciously we know it as the closest physical experience we can have of the Beloved.

In moments of intense pleasure, of maximum fulfillment, the relentless chatter in our minds, the constant planning, scheming and fantasizing of our egos, cease. We become so completely absorbed in the pleasure of the moment that we slip temporarily out of time and into peace. Even conventional orgasm gives the mind a brief, temporary lapse of thought. In that narrow and sacred window of orgasmic experience we peek into the rapturous, supremely fulfilled, substratum of the mind. Herein lays the deepest spiritual intent behind sexual communion, behind the whole art and science of lovemaking.

A moment comes when we no longer yearn for sex, when we simply rest in the stillness of the Beloved. From a spiritual perspective sex is but a jumping off point to pure meditative mind, to mind resting contented in its own unbounded nature.

The Tantric sages who explored the depths of sexual energy were fully integrated in love; every moment they were united with the Beloved. They recognized the futility of trying to suppress desire. These sages saw with immense insight and compassion that desire appears to lead the mind away from the Self. But they also recognized that the very nature of desire is to somehow return to the Self. Desire is always in search of happiness, and therefore the Self. Through contemplation, the Tantric sages realized that no other desire is held captive in the human mind the way sexual desire is. Therefore sex must be one of the most powerful keys to Self-discovery. The sages investigated sex as a science and practiced it as a spiritual art.

12. In Sexual Communion We are Honoring Desire—As we bring heartfelt awareness into the act, we turn a potentially vulgar experience into one of immense purity. Our bodies relax. Our minds become pristine and quiet. We experience a level of intimacy with our partners that transcends words. Intimacy puts an end to alienation and the violence that can arise from it. Unlike the agitation that often accompanies more conventional sex, in sexual communion the whole mind/body organism becomes calm and peaceful.

David says: My wife, Faye, has taught this old yogi that desire is never the enemy of life. When we listen carefully, desire is the way home.

13. Love and Do What Thou Will is the Whole of the Law—Certainly there are important sexual techniques we can integrate into the sexual experience with our partner. But we miss the essence of sexual communion when we strategize in some way to maximize our pleasure. Strategizing always involves a certain level of control, and control is founded on fear. Sexual communion is based on the opposite of fear: love.

As the heart releases unconscious guilt, resentment, and fear, a reverence for all beings arises. We do not have to try and be compassionate. With the experience of our own innocence our behavior spontaneously reflects greater kindness and care toward others. There is no need to plan or contemplate our words or behavior when the heart is saturated in love. Love and do what thou will. Or, in the words of the Japanese Zen Master, Bunan:

Die while you're alive and be absolutely dead.
Then do whatever you want: it's all good.

THE ART OF BREATHING

Awareness of the breath is fundamental to sexual communion. Conscious breathing opens the body, stills the mind, and develops concentration. Breath circulates energy and intensifies pleasure. It stimulates shakti and strengthens sexual endurance. Awareness and breath are what we refer to as the King and Queen of healing, especially sexual communion.

There are virtually hundreds of yogic breathing techniques to explore. But for our purposes we want to share just two methods that are easy, enjoyable, and at the same very healing for couples.

THE HARMONIZING BREATH

Lie down together like spoons, front to back, and simply take long deep breaths in rhythm with each other for ten or fifteen minutes. Breathing is the easiest and most direct way to immediately harmonize your energies. If you are tired it will recharge your battery. If you are out of synch it will help to harmonize you.

We call this the *Harmonizing Breath*, and you can do it before you make love, during lovemaking, before bed, or anytime you just want to snuggle and hang out together. Just do slow deep breaths through the nose together, in the same rhythm.

THE GIVING AND RECEIVING BREATH

We recommend this breathing technique at various times during lovemaking while you are still together, when you have either just backed off the orgasm, or following orgasm while you are resting in each other's arms. We will use Scott and Linda to help us explain this technique.

Engaged in intercourse, they begin breathing in opposite rhythm. While Scott exhales, Linda inhales. While Linda inhales, Scott exhales. As Scott inhales, he visualizes drawing energy in through his genitals. Linda visualizes sending Scott energy through hers on her exhale. As Scott exhales, he visualizes sending Linda energy through his heart to her heart. As she inhales, she visualizes the drawing in of energy to her heart from his. Again, when Linda exhales she sends Scott energy through her vagina. And as he inhales, he draws in the energy through his penis. Now again he circulates the energy back to her through his heart on the exhale.

We can also circulate the energy in the opposite direction. That is, on the inhale Scott visualizes receiving energy in his chest from Linda's heart. Then on the exhale he visualizes sending energy to Linda through his penis into her vagina as she simultaneously inhales. Again, on the exhale she sends energy through her heart. Scott receives it on his inhale and sends it back to her through his penis as he exhales.

This Giving and Receiving Breath is good to do anytime you make love. You are circulating the psychic energy or shakti generated by your sexual fires through your chakras and into one another. Such breath work is very bonding, healing, and mutually energizing. It is especially good to do for a few minutes after male ejaculation. It allows for the male to replenish the chi, or shakti, that was released during orgasm.

SEXUAL COMMUNION AND COMPASSION FOR THE WORLD

Can our love for one another be transformed into compassion for the world? Sexual communion teaches us that it can. When we learn to open fully to one person, we open to all. It is from this realization that sages throughout the world proclaim: *The World Is My Family!* The path of spiritual partnership begins by learning to love each other and our families deeply. As our love grows, the heart extends out to our community, culture, country, world, and finally—so the sages tell us—to the cosmos.

DAILY SEXUAL COMMUNION: AN EXERCISE IN INTIMACY

We have discovered that a powerful way to deepen intimacy and strengthen the bond between us is to make love regularly, even daily for a period of time. For couples who are ready to accelerate and deepen their intimacy, we recommend the following exercise.

Make love daily for twenty-one days, allowing two hours each day for sexual intimacy. At the same time, take all the emphasis off the need to orgasm. Simply stay stimulated enough to remain sexually connected. Avoid movement as much as possible. Just be with one another in sexual embrace. Maintain as much eye contact as possible. Feel free to verbalize, but say nothing that might be combative. Breathe tunefully with one another. Be meditative. See how present you can be. When you break sexual contact at the end, just lay quietly together in each other's arms for sometime before finally arising.

Daily sexual communion can be very powerful for couples and frequently brings up emotional material. As you engage in the above practice, notice whether resistance arises at various points along the way. Why might either of you want to avoid intimacy? Is there something that needs to be expressed? Is there fear centered on the heart, or solar plexus? The healing power of daily lovemaking has to do with bringing a strong presence into the moment. Presence grows with our capacity to open to the moment free of judgment.

THE WEDDING DANCE

The sexual dance is a mirror of our relationship to the Beloved. We begin with the awareness of our separateness but in the process become one. In this dance, we shed not only our outer clothes but more importantly our inner ones as well. As we open to one another, heart and mind are exposed and gradually united in the process. In Taoist teachings of China, this union is referred to as the Marriage of Heaven and Earth. Masculine (heaven) and feminine (earth) energies unify, and our vision, which once saw only duality, now sees only wholeness.

CHAPTER NINE

The Essence

We've come into the presence of the One
Who was never apart from us.
—RUMI

It is clear why many great masters, thinkers, and artists choose the path of relationship as a potent metaphor for coming home to essence. The male/female dance is the dynamic interplay of interconnected opposites, of masculine/ feminine, rational/intuitive, aggressive/receptive, warm/cool, solar/lunar. It is on the passionate, metaphorical stage of intimate relationships that spirit dances in chaos, magic and mystery. In our most human love we are shattered and made whole constantly by a divine force infinitely more powerful than our minds. Love says: Listen to the essence beyond words! Speak from the essence that nourishes the heart and soul of things! It is the essence of the *Invisible Wedding* that we will explore in this final chapter.

WHAT IS AT THE CORE OF AN
INVISIBLE WEDDING?

Following are fifteen key principles that express the core teachings on spiritual partnerships.

1. The Invisible Wedding is the Weaving Together of Each Person's Inner Wholeness—There is a poignant section in the New Testament when Jesus turns water into wine at the wedding feast of Canna. The wedding is a spiritual metaphor for wholeness, for the inner alchemical weaving together of masculine/feminine energies in the enlightened state. It is a symbol for the reawakening of wisdom, integration, and truth.

Water becoming wine is symbolic of consciousness as we evolve from a state of suffering in duality to one of freedom in unity. The spiritual purpose behind marriage is to help mend the inner split between heart and mind, between the feminine and masculine, and thereby come home to the realization of our essential wholeness.

Our partners become powerful mirrors of our inner opposites. We find we cannot be intimate with each other without connecting with these deeper parts of our selves. This is the yoga of spiritual partnership. Lovers diving deep into the heart naturally become more poetic, intuitive, creative and wholesome.

2. In the Dance of Intimacy Our Partners Become Exquisite Reflections of Our Subconscious—This is one of the most profound principles of spiritual relationship, and it can be one of the most difficult to act upon because that which we find most unacceptable about them is the thing we most need to accept within ourselves During times of disagreement and conflict we have a tendency to blame our partners for our inner discomfort. The truth is, at such times our partners are mirroring a neglected aspect of our own subconscious, which is in need of acceptance. Such acceptance is part of the fire of purification that starts to burn in true intimacy.

There are no accidents when it comes to who we attract for partnership. We are attracted to a partner who fits closely enough the portrait of our inner mate. Carl Jung referred to our inner male/female as animus/anima. A good deal of Jungian psychology explores the nature of these inner opposites and how we project them onto various figures in our lives, both personally and collectively. Sages have known about this phenomenon since the beginning of time.

Invariably, we begin to work out any unresolved parental issues with our spouses. In this lifetime it is our parents who have the most powerful influence in the shaping of our subconscious characters. When it comes to choosing partners, it is the opposite sex parent who carries the most influence (especially in first marriages). Males tend to choose partners who fit the mother pattern, and females tend to choose partners who fit the father pattern. The key word is *pattern*. On the surface our spouses can seem very different from our parents, but the subconscious reads the pattern, not the obvious traits or features. Unfinished business with that parent will eventually seek completion through the marriage, as we project unresolved issues with our parents onto our partners.

Our partners give us the precious gift of allowing us to come to a greater self-understanding. They reflect ourselves back to us in a way that no one else can. As we learn to accept our mates for who they really are, including all their worst faults, we come to a deeper level of self-acceptance. This does

not mean we have to like or approve of everything they do—
or everything we do. What acceptance means is that we are
able to remain open in our hearts. Staying open for each other,
is staying open to ourselves.

Every relationship has an unconscious healing agenda. The
deepest level of healing reveals this: At the deepest level of the
Self, there is no other.

**3. Realizing Our Inherent Happiness Lies Only in the
Beloved (God, or Self), Partners Cannot be Responsible for Each
Other's Happiness**—There is no ultimate happiness outside the
Self, or the Beloved. Realizing this relieves our relationships of
the terrible burden of being responsible for each other's hap
piness. It is the tendency of the mind to seek happiness outside
its own nature. The meditative traditions refer to this tendency
as the monkey mind, since the mind is constantly leaping from
one object to another searching for perfect happiness. There is
no perfect happiness outside the Self. Call It God. Call It Wisdom. Call It Wholeness. Call It the Beloved.

Relationships cannot give us anything—neither pleasure
nor pain—that we do not already have within ourselves. In the
words of the Japanese master Zenrin: If you do not get it from
yourself, where will you go for it?

**4. Allow Disillusionment to be a Masterful Teacher During
Times of Loss and Setbacks**—Because it forces you to turn
within. There was a time in childhood when we were aware of
our intrinsic happiness. We were safe in our bodies, and we
knew that we were loved. It did not matter that there was conflict at home, or that our parents got angry. We were still living
primarily in our hearts, not our judging minds.

Thus, everything was well in our world because all was well within. As our egos gradually came into play—and with this the budding of the rational mind—the feeling of wholeness began to fade. The feeling of unity gradually gave way to one of separation and the disturbing sense that we were not loved. This stage in life marks a fundamental (though only notional) break with our native life-force, our link with source, our Beloved.

From that point forward, the mind searches restlessly for that special feeling of well-being that comes with being loved. We pursue relationships of all types looking for that special someone or something—sky diving, meditation, drugs, power, money—to turn us on again.

Falling in love always begins with the incredible sense of being loved—and a dramatic increase in energy and well-being. We feel bright, happy, healthy, and alert. Once again we feel connected within to our source. Once again all is well in our world because all is well within. We feel loved. But we attribute this feeling to the other—and this is the grand illusion. In romance we project our unconscious Self-love (that which was repressed in the formation of our egos) onto our new lover. But falling in love is only a replica of that original experience of feeling unconditionally loved and at home within.

Like a built-in homing device implanted by God, we have a natural urge to be in love, connected to essence. Romance can be a doorway to this essence in the heart, but typically our hearts get broken first. Disillusionment—and the disappointment that follows—is simply that point on the journey where once again we begin to lose the nourishing feeling of being unified. Instead of being the source of love, our partner becomes the cause of our suffering. Usually something is said or done by one of us that runs counter to an emotional need of the other, and suddenly our defenses riot and our separateness returns. Only now it is magnified because we contrast our disillusionment with the recent high of romance. This is why lovers' quarrels can be so intense. Disillusionment is a junction point that can either intensify our suffering or release us, depending on our awareness.

It is at this turning point that we may be tempted to project our disappointment onto our partner. Instead, we need to keep in touch with our feeling of disappointment and feel it as deeply as possible, experiencing it in all its naked qualities. The mind will try every trick it knows to run from this moment. It will argue, blame, project, spin out, justify and conceptualize. It will seek another object (a new partner) for its gratification. But we must not veer from our commitment to look within ourselves. It is in such raw moments of vulnerability that love can bloom. Disappointment can encourage the mind to turn inward, leading our awareness back to the primal wound of abandonment and broken-heartedness, where separation was first woven into the fabric of our experience. When we allow ourselves to experience this level of awareness, life-energy is released—and our fear turns to a feeling of love. In this way, disillusionment, like romance, can become a doorway into the heart. When welcomed, it delivers us to a place deep inside, to our true essence. From essence we realize that we do not need a partner to be content, peaceful, in love. We are all these in essence.

Eventually we will begin to feel loved again but in a whole new way. For the first time perhaps, we will be able to reach out to life with real openness and receptivity, rather than fear and wanting. When we do, we discover a new sanity within our relationships. We approach things with an open, gracious, big heart. We stop grasping for something external and rediscover our completely natural sense of wholeness. Wholeness is the only basis of a genuine loving relationship, allowing us to come together with the spontaneous desire to give and nurture.

Disillusionment is life's way of waking us up and driving us inward, where we discover that we have always been loved—that we are born into love, grow into love, and die into love.

5. Confront the Emotional Shadows that Create Conflict in Your Life—Cultivating intimacy is a process of letting down our defenses, and when we do so the pain that was being protected comes out into the open. In this sense, lovers often get more than they consciously bargain for. While spiritual partners can't help but undergo crises throughout their lives, love is a purifying agent.

A woman who was sexually abused as a child might suddenly feel the urge to run rather than face into a deeper level of intimacy with her partner. The urge to bolt can go on for months, even years, before it finally dissolves. A man who as a young boy watched his mother continually criticize his father might suddenly feel anger toward his partner for an unintentional comment. All manner of emotional vulnerability can arise in the context of deepened intimacy. The root of conflict is always the ego, the feeling of being separate and unloved.

The sense of not feeling loved arises from duality and causes fear. When we follow the path of fear we perpetuate more conflict to support our premise of not being loved. When we follow the path of love, conflict dissolves, because we come into our wholeness, our unity.

Conflict can be an opportunity to deepen our sense of wholeness, by bringing to light our shadow side and thus mending our sense of separateness. Rather than suppressing conflict, we can realize that nothing is intrinsically an obstacle to peace, that we are never permanently damaged. Once we completely integrate love into our being, we have no choice but to turn to love. A rose has no choice but to be a rose. A person who loses her separateness has no choice but to love life.

6. Wise Lovers First Embrace, then Release Emotions. Like Clouds, They Come and Go—It is important to understand our emotions, to get safe with them, to experience them in their naked qualities. But it is also important to remember that we are not in essence what we feel. Emotions are like clouds in the sky; when we open into them all the way—when we embrace them whole-heartedly—we come out the other side realizing that they are temporary and insubstantial. Our original Buddha nature is the vastness of the sky. Thoughts, feelings, events rise and fall away. But our basic nature remains the same.

The trap we may fall into when dealing with our emotions is identifying with our anger or fear or jealousy to the extent that we define ourselves by that feeling. When this is the case, we no longer just feel anger—we are anger. We no longer feel jealous—we are jealous. Our perspective narrows and we lose sight of what we really are. It would be like the ocean forgetting its vastness and believing it is merely a wave.

When we invest too much in our emotions, they can seem more real and important than they are. We are aided in this way of thinking by much of modern psychology, which fails to acknowledge the soul or spiritual Self. The awakening of the Self, however, allows us to recognize the realms of mind, body and emotion without losing sight of our spiritual core.

It is important to be able to process our emotional material. But as a part of this process we must also learn to let go. Find the place inside that does not change. The deeper truth is that we are not our emotions.

7. Love is More Important than Worldly Status, and it Will Grow and Flourish like a Well-tended Garden when You Make it Your Priority—Making our relationship a priority means that we do not allow our worldly goals and interests to be fulfilled at the expense of our commitment to one another. Relative to other commitments in our lives, harmony between us comes first.

The path of spiritual partnership reveals that love of God comes first, then my partner, then our children, then the other things of the world. Better yet, visualize the sacred triangle with husband and wife at the base and the Beloved (or Truth) at the apex. Regular meditation, prayer, and various other forms of inner work can come into play here, but only when used to investigate reality and not as self-protective devises and defense mechanisms against emotional contact.

In a spiritual partnership one's inner work is not something that is separate from the art of relating. Personal and interpersonal transformations mirror each other. What we experience internally in our meditations or other moments of personal healing will naturally be reflected in our relationships. Staying present in our relationship is certainly no less important than meditating regularly. It might even be much more important. A true spiritual experience will bear the gift of greater generosity and love toward others.

What is the greatest gift of intimacy? Life itself. As we embrace each other, we embrace life. When we nurture our relationship, when we abandon our exit strategies and really commit to being present for each other, the fire of transformation starts to burn. Old outworn core beliefs surface for investigation and release.

The spirit of love purifies the various knots in our hearts, allowing us to open deeper to each other and the world around us.

A highly successful man came to us for counseling because he was feeling very depressed. Having sold his business at forty-five, he had recently achieved all his financial goals. But his feelings of depression left him seriously questioning the cost of his financial freedom. For many years he had worked twelve to fourteen hour days, seven days a week, at his business. While he compulsively chased his dream of financial freedom his children grew up and his wife went through many life changes alone, without him. One day, out of the blue, she called him into their bedroom and told him she was filing for divorce. There was no room for discussion, no possibility of reconciliation. The subject was closed. At that moment this man suddenly confronted the hollowness of his ambition. He began to uncover the underlying emotional insecurity that had ruthlessly driven him for so many of his adult years.

In the days that followed, he told us that his "heart broke into a thousand pieces" as he realized the finality of his wife's decision and that no amount of change or promise on his part was sufficient to put their lives back together again. It was a time of fierce grace. Over the next few months this gentleman turned inward. He saw that he had to find his own heart within himself before he could hope to create a healthy relationship with anyone else. It would take some time before he stopped applying the same ambitious drive toward his spirituality as he had toward his business success, but he was on a steady path. He knew from the painful school of heartbreak the awful price of putting material desires above matters of the heart, of staying unconscious to the beautiful force of love that had supported him faithfully all through his life. On the positive side, his suffering caused him to begin his healing. He came to see the divorce as a real blessing. It caused his heart to break open.

8. In the Dance of Intimacy Our True Relationship is with the Beloved—Our relationship with our partner—no matter how sublime, joyous, and nurturing—is ultimately a metaphor for the inner wedding. It can never take the place of our relationship to the Beloved within.

In less conscious forms of relating, each partner looks to the other for reinforcement of self-image or ego. Out of fear, partners attempt to manipulate each other into giving what is lacking within—things like appreciation and approval. Partners do this to avoid deep-seated feelings and core-beliefs of inadequacy. Such relationships end up creating the very fear-based states of mind they are trying to avoid. In a spiritual partnership the emphasis always falls back on the inner work, the deepening of our own centers. We encourage each other to look within, to expose subconscious core-beliefs and to cultivate our own essential self.

We realize that we cannot give our partners what each of us must ultimately work out on the inside. Inner qualities such as self-worth, self-esteem, courage, independence, endurance, and emotional maturity come from our own inner work and from facing up to our own difficult lessons and life challenges. Certainly we grow in the context of our relationship, but as we become more conscious we recognize that nobody can integrate our lessons for us. In fact, when help becomes a means of avoiding pain, it is a hindrance to our growth.

In a spiritual partnership we have enough faith in each other to allow ourselves to make mistakes, to test out our wings, to explore our strengths and weaknesses, and to wrestle with our own inner pain without the need to be rescued. We learn to let go of control. Or rather, we recognize that we do not have control.

What are some spiritual strategies that each partner can use to begin to find comfort within them? To strengthen their own inner core, men must let go of the neurotic need for female nurturing. When they feel inclined to lean emotionally on their partners or other female friends, knowing it is more appropriate to handle this need themselves, they can go for a jaunt in nature, meditate, or seek out a male friend. This tendency to lean too heavily on women is a throw-back to childhood nursing tendencies; too many men still try and handle their sense of insecurity by going to the breast for comfort.

A man's healing journey usually brings him face-to-face with many figures, but at some point his father will stand out. Men can become overly dependent on women when not receiving the proper support from their fathers as youngsters. They unconsciously identify women as safe, primary sources of emotional support. This places an enormous burden on their mates. Men must find ways of nurturing the wholeness within themselves.

Occasional ventures into the wilds can help men stay both grounded and centered. The elements have a powerful healing effect on us. A meditation retreat can also guide us inward and strengthen our centers. Or we can sit, eyes and ears open, in the center of our emotional fire, without doing anything special.

A woman's healing involves finding her approval within, instead of from a man. She must look to her own heart for love, support, and appreciation. When she enters a relationship from her center, she gives only what can be received. And she receives only what is given in love. She nurtures without being drained. And she receives support without becoming dependent. She is able to establish healthy boundaries. In nurturing her essence within, she naturally protects her heart from predators who unconsciously seek wholeness at her expense. And she is able to open to healthy, supportive males, who approach her with the desire to give, rather than take.

Once women accept responsibility for their own well-being, they no longer play victim to male domination. They also no longer are inclined to use men's emotional insecurities to try and raise their self-esteem by giving in ways that foster dependency. They come to the realization that nobody can stand between them and their own personal relationship with God—no priest, no guru, no husband, no employer, nothing but their own minds. Only from this strong, sacred space inside can their voices give expression to truth. And their truth is important. The truth arising from a woman's deep intuition is something that family and society need desperately today.

When we stand tall in our own circles there is a natural tolerance for the differences and spaces between us. We do not have to reach consensus over every matter to be comfortable with ourselves. We accept each other's natures. Standing in our circles does not mean that we fortify ourselves from life, or that we live within such boundaries that we are unable to nurture or be nurtured by our spouses. It means internal freedom. We begin opening and closing according to our own intuitive wisdom. We come from our center. When centered we are more relaxed, peaceful and aware. Generosity and tolerance arise naturally and appropriately when the heart and mind are peaceful.

The greatest gift we can share with our partner is the deep, vibrant presence that is an expression of the Self, the Beloved.

9. The Art of Successful Communication is Born from a Still Heart and a Meditative Mind—As we become more conscious, we begin to comprehend that the whole universe is about communication. Everything is alive, connected and dancing. At a quantum level the boundaries are fluid and transparent.

Communication is about making contact. Acknowledging and sharing our "heavy" states of mind, like fear, anger, and sadness, add substance to the overall pattern of our evolving relationship.

Real communication affirms the unity underlying our differing individual desires and predilections. It creates space to be what we are. It uncovers the positive intention behind our actions, even those that seem misguided at times. True communication is an opening into just what is, to whatever is arising in the moment. We are not required to be what we are not or to say what is untrue. Sometimes silence is the most powerful form of communication.

The real secret to communication is in our quiet, uncluttered, meditative mind. A meditative mind is one free of judgment and comparison. When the mind holds no judgment it functions from a state of inner quiet and peace. It no longer barks like a dog when it comes up against some perceived threat from the outside world.

A meditative mind touches upon that substratum of intelligence that is intuitively connected to everyone else; thus, it is the true basis for communication. Communication works best when we are not attached to the outcome of our action. A calm, meditative mind is fundamentally at peace with any outcome, so it supports the expression of all other points of view. It doesn't mind being wrong or fuss over being right. A meditative mind is not attached to any position and is therefore the ultimate negotiator. It is laser-like in that it allows us to focus intensely without losing perspective.

At the deepest moments of sharing, we might ask ourselves, "Is it my partner I am in touch with, or is it me? Or has the small 'i' become big 'I.' " As Carl Jung remarked once:

> On a collective level we are no longer separate individuals, we are all one. . . . The basic structure of the mind is the same in everybody.

When communication dives vertically we sometimes get the sense that the space between our bodies has been bridged. It is as if our bodies are no longer defining or limiting who we are. Beyond even this it is as if our minds, with all their concepts, judgments, and opinions, become empty and thus are no longer defining us or limiting who and what we are. We are just present for whatever wants to happen. In that moment communication has evolved into communion.

When we are in communion lovemaking is no longer confined to physical intercourse but finds expression in the simplest of things—the tone of voice, a mere glance, a touch on the shoulder. Even anger and the so-called shadow emotions find voices that somehow affirm the truth and basic innocence of our natures. They become just different forces of nature, like wind, thunder, and lightning. Nothing sticks. Nothing is denied. Nothing is restricted. Real communication (communion) gives expression to the widest possible love, which ultimately accepts whatever is, judging and condemning nothing.

10. Listen to the Inner Feminine Voice. It Plays a Vital Role in Creating Peace Within Yourself, Your Relationship, and the Community—The world has been under the oppressive gun of patriarchy for several thousand years. Women have suffered most, but everyone is wounded. When women are subjugated the whole world suffers. The masculine intellect, without the balance of intuitive feeling, is like moving through space with a huge, bloated head. Western European culture has been lurching along like this for centuries. It has trampled and destroyed Nature around the world and poisoned all the simple earth-based cultures it has touched. Fortunately, balance is slowly being restored by the tapping into of our feminine energy. The feminine is the doorway to God.

The old wisdom teachings from India, Tibet, North and South America and native cultures around the world tell us that women have much to offer in the way of intuitive wisdom. Love of the Divine Mother is the oldest form of worship, and devotion to Her is awakening throughout the world. More than ever today, the world needs the qualities of motherhood.

Women represent the lunar, intuitive, nurturing aspects of life. The feminine aspect of us has greater access to intuitive knowledge, which extends far beyond the conscious rational mind. In a spiritual partnership each person is renewed by opening to the other. As a woman opens fully to her supportive male partner she simultaneously attunes with her masculine side. She finds a strength and confidence in asserting herself and also in being more deeply receptive. As a man opens fully to his supportive female partner his capacity to give from the heart expands, and he learns to trust in receptivity. He discovers the art of listening and thus becomes more tolerant and compassionate in his approach to living. Both genders are able to give and receive an abundance of nurturing, strengthening each other and the relationship as a whole.

We can do a lot for world peace right now if we simply bring our homes into balance. For this to happen, women must reclaim their spirituality. In all the great wisdom traditions a woman is recognized as the embodiment of great shakti, or power. A man is never diminished in his heartfelt worship of the feminine. On the contrary, he is made whole. As a woman shines in her spirituality she naturally turns her partner's energies to the love of the Beloved. When both partners face God, the home shines with the pure light of devotion. Children remain connected to the joy of life, and their hearts grow naturally in fullness as they mature.

The Yoni Tantra, a sacred scripture from India, states, "Women are divinity, women are life, women are truly jewels . . . every woman is thought of as a manifestation of the Goddess."

Wherever disaster strikes, we find women cleaning up in the wake; nursing the wounded, sweeping up the streets, mending the broken-hearted. It is time to honor the women for their sacred roles as healers of life. From Lao Tzu:

The Tao is called the Great Mother:
empty yet inexhaustible
it gives birth to infinite worlds.
It is always present within you.
You can use it any way you want.

The feminine is the doorway to the heart, and the heart is where we meet the Beloved. It is for this reason that women in all the ancient societies were worshipped, honored, and respected. They embody most potently the feminine principle which takes us to God.

11. The Sacred Art of Sexual Communion Helps Rebalance Masculine/Feminine Energies Allowing Men to Become More Visionary and Intuitive, and Women to Find Their Confidence—

When sex is practiced consciously a doorway is open to our interior lives. Healing forces in the subconscious find release. The fire of intimacy purifies fears, misunderstandings, and blockages in our bodies. We come into balance.

Masculine/feminine energies complete one another. Where is the intuitive without the logical for balance? Where is the logical without the intuitive for balance? Wisdom arises from the playful mingling of these opposites. Nowhere are these interconnected opposites livelier than in the playful, erotic dance between a man and woman.

When a man orgasms inside his partner, polarities suddenly shift. In that moment she gains his masculine (yang) energy and he moves into the feminine (yin) energy. She becomes full and he becomes empty. In this way lovers move back and forth with their energies and explore all points in between in the conscious art of lovemaking. Some men resist this feeling of being empty; as it has to do with being out of control. Yet emptiness is the basis of fullness. It is the power behind the world of form and the essence of meditation.

In conscious sexual communion we might sometimes choose to postpone male orgasm to explore the full range of possibilities before us, to go deeper into our communion. We use awareness and breath to circulate energies to all parts of our bodies and to guide us into more profound levels of intimacy with each other, and ultimately with ourselves. Our sexual dance becomes a springboard for awakening our interior lives. Prolonged love-making allows each partner the opportunity to absorb each one's essence. The male connects with his feminine counterpart, gaining the power of nurturance and intuition in the process. The female connects with her masculine side, gaining the power of focus, confidence, and voice in the process.

The force of shakti opens our chakras through lovemaking. Sex becomes life-giving, rejuvenating, creative, and deeply bonding.

Shakti is the sacred healing energy represented since the time of the Greeks as the Caduceus, the two snakes winding up the staff of life, or the spinal column of the human nervous system.

When our chakras open to each other in lovemaking we ex-change subtle, powerful, and healing energies. Latent energies in the subconscious are stirred and spontaneously transmitted to our partners. In this sexual dance, we share our deepest essences with each other and bond at the level of each chakra that gets enlivened.

Through conventional sex we share primarily at the level of the first three charkas, since the base chakras get enlivened with or without conscious awareness. The lower chakras have to do with survival, self-identity and power. When we engage in sexual communion we consciously circulate our energies upward throughout our entire systems. Thus we can channel the shakti generated by the sexual dance to open the heart, throat, third-eye and crown chakras, where we share at deep spiritual levels.

As we keep going deeper into the sexual dance—periodically relaxing and circulating our energy so the male does not or-gasm quickly— we tap into more profound levels of spiritual energy and awareness. A man finds the ability to orgasm without loss of semen. Sex becomes a window through which we glimpse the inherently blissful, ecstatic nature of the Beloved. We can use this opportunity to become meditative.

Conventional modes of sexual intercourse are full of heat and passion but include very little quiet time. Thus, orgasm comes intensely and quickly. In this context orgasm is like a good sneeze, or scratching an itch; the experience lacks depth and subtlety. In sexual communion we bring our presence—through relaxation, calmness, and silence—into the dance. We can make love for hours if we want, allowing our sexual passion to rise and fall many times. We find that we can ride all aspects of the wave with greater intensity and awareness simply by remaining present. Men can experience waves of orgasmic energy many times without losing themselves. Women can let go fully into the experience, having multiple orgasms if they want because of the attunement between them and their partners. But even here, silence is the real cauldron from which everything else emerges.

When a woman orgasms the male receives a powerful hit of shakti. This is one of the many secret gifts that a woman gives to a man. When she is turned on shakti pours through her nipples and fingers. In sexual communion we give and receive energy on countless unseen levels. And in this way we move into deeper alignment with one another and ourselves. Through sexual communion a man learns to trust his feminine side; he becomes receptive. Through sexual communion a woman learns to trust her voice; she becomes more confident. Both learn to open deeper to the other, and thus to life.

When we experience boredom in our sexual life it is often due to emotional resistance. We are afraid to surrender deeper into the unknown territory of the heart. Communicating our fears can help remove such distance. Staying conscious (alert and present) during lovemaking is another way through the wall of fear. We have to trust that the positive intention of the moment will set the two of us free of our self-imposed inhibitions. Love is not for the shy and weak hearted. It will eventually strip us of our need for control. Boredom will eventually yield through honest, loving attention.

It is important to communicate any grievances that might be registered in the heart. Choose a suitable time—not during lovemaking—to share any past hurts.

One of the greatest gifts a man can give a woman is a genuine listening heart, even if it requires him to touch profound levels of pain. One of the greatest gifts a woman can give a man is let him know that he is truly loved regardless of how well he performs.

The mystery of love continues revealing itself. There is no end to how much we can enjoy together. Our natures are infinite and finally unknowable. In this dance, both partners must learn to give to each other without the need for something in return.

Couples who engage in conscious sexual communion become happier and more balanced within themselves. As a result they naturally express more positive qualities to the people around them.

Imagine the life-supporting effect if national leaders took sacred time to make deep and harmonious love with their spouses before making important decisions!

12. When the Heart is Filled with Songs of Love, Praise, and Gratitude, There is Nothing to Fear—In an intimate relationship, especially in times of disillusionment, we must consciously avoid giving too much attention to the negativity that arises. We want to learn to handle what arises as efficiently as possible, and let it go.

Sometimes, due to a backlog of suppressed pain from childhood, a healing crisis can be of such intensity that we lose perspective on the purpose of our spiritual partnership—which is the expansion of wholeness. Here are a few things to keep in mind when facing such a crisis:

First: Remember that behind every action, no matter how strange or disturbing it may be, lies a positive intention. The basic impulse behind every thought is the expansion of love and happiness. When the innocent impulses of the heart become distorted, it is due to our fears.

Second: Our partners are often mirrors of the hidden parts of us that we have difficulty facing. Show gratitude to your partner for revealing those things to you. Thank her or him for their commitment to you. It is rare in this life to be truly loved.

Third: It is a spiritual law that what we place our attention on the most grows. When we find our awareness focusing on the negative, either in ourselves or others, we can gently bring it back to the ascending attitudes. No one has died from love, praise, or gratitude. There is a saying in *The Upanishads*:

> Let us be together
> Let us eat together
> Let us be radiating truth,
> Radiating the light of life.
> Never shall we denounce anyone,
> Never entertain negativity.

As your partner shares authentic, positive perceptions of you, notice if there are any areas in your body that become tense. Close your eyes and bring your awareness into any discomforts that might arise. These sensations are part of the healing process. Breathe into them and know that the God in you and the God in your partner love you unconditionally. Can you handle this much love?

We have seen many relationships over the years die because of an over-emphasis on negativity and the processing of emotional garbage. Such a focus may well be appropriate during times of disillusionment, but always the emphasis must be on getting back to the positive values. When couples become addicted to conflict they forget the higher dharma and purpose of their being together, which is the raising of our spiritual vision toward the Beloved.

As we unfold spiritually we come to realize that nothing in life can be taken for granted, least of all the people we love. Each breath may be our last. If we knew that we only had seventy-two hours to live, how would it change our attitude? Awareness would get focused very quickly. Chances are our hearts would simply want to share love, praise and gratitude.

13. The Path of Love is a Process of Shifting from the Personal to the Universal—In a conscious relationship the question eventually arises: How can we serve?

Once we are bonded and have had the time to nurture our intimacy through adequate sexual play, emotional sharing, and spiritual rapport, it is vital that we offer service to a cause beyond our intimate relationship with each other.

For many couples this urge finds expression in raising a family. For others it might involve a social service like teaching or healing work. Serving can be any activity that marks a turning outward, an offering of ourselves to others. The important thing is that we find ways to give beyond our primary relationship.

If we live within the cocoon of our relationship, it is as if Mother Nature puts the breaks on our growth. We suffocate. There is a natural law working here that requires us to give back outwardly and equally what we have been given. Our experience is that we cannot receive anymore until we let go of what we have. Our relationship will suffer if we do not give our love to a bigger cause.

A genuine spiritual partnership is never focused on self-gratification. It will continuously point us in the direction of greater wholeness, totality, and integration. This means that if our relationship is truly founded on spiritual principles it will lead us in a direction away from selfish tendencies. But this is not forced. Love—if it is love—eventually supports others and opens us to many facets of life.

When all is said and done for this life and our Maker awaits us, it probably won't matter a hoot how much money we have accrued, how much fame and power were ours, or how many awards we received; it will just be a matter of heart.

Crazy Horse, the Lakota Medicine Man and warrior, used to have a saying before going into battle: "Today is a good day to die!" What he must have meant by this was that his heart was clear. He was at peace with his Maker. He wasn't hiding or rejecting anything. He was coming from his center, in full acceptance of what his life presented. He was transparent and fully present.

St. Paul expressed essentially the same idea when he taught that we must die daily in Christ. To die daily is to live fully in the present moment.

It is a wonderful spiritual law that the more we give to life the more life gives back. As we take the necessary steps in our relationship to follow Spirit, even when we are frightened and it seems we have to let go our grip of each other, the universe somehow provides for us.

14. Our Love for the Beloved Embodies Unconditional Love and Freedom—Although love for the Beloved will eventually outshine the love for each other, it is the beginning of unconditional love and freedom.

Sooner or later a yearning can arise from deep within the heart for something more than our relationship. We may even feel guilty about it. But this yearning is a blessing, not a curse. It is the beginning of a deeper love, a love that is not dependent on an other for fulfillment. To the mind this yearning can feel like death, and we may even fear that the relationship is dying. All that is actually dying is our selfish attachment to each other. The Beloved is consuming our ignorance. It is calling us home to the heart, where love is simply what we are.

15. A Spiritual Partnership Reveals that Love is the Simple Acceptance of What is, and with Acceptance Comes Freedom—By now it should be clear that in our definition of love we are not trying to create a paradise without pain. What we're point ing to is a wedding of heaven and earth. Love forces us to address pain, aggression and ugliness, as well as the golden beauty of the world. There is nothing to reject.

The acceptance of whatever arises has become the theme of our work with couples over the last twenty years. Most couples who come to see us are on some kind of spiritual journey already. They wouldn't naturally be drawn to us otherwise. Still, there is often the stubborn conditioning that life ought to be different than it is. He shouldn't be so withdrawn. It shouldn't be so painful. We should have more money. We should make love more often. He ought to take better care of himself. We shouldn't fight so much. If only we didn't get angry. He shouldn't eye other women. She shouldn't be attracted to other males. Our judgments are in constant battle with reality. Like barking dogs at night, they refuse to let us rest. But life can be very messy. We're utterly human, with all the contradictions and confusions that come with the deal. Our relationship inevitably reflects all our states of mind. Yet it also reflects our essence.

Eventually we have to enter the moment, because this is the only place where life is happening. In the moment we come to simple acceptance. We accept our limitations, judgments, core-beliefs, and all the heavy states of mind and body.

Love is continually evolving, breaking boundaries, and finding new forms of expression. It does not fit into a neat conventional box. It obeys a higher law. It flows according to its will, not ours. With acceptance comes inner freedom.

Secrecy, control, and hidden agendas have no place in the shared heart. The two of us have gone through all our major ordeals in life together, with nothing hidden or withheld. There is plenty we do not know, but this much we can say: True spiritual partnership thrives on transparency—the simple, naked truth.

> *Love gives naught but itself*
> *and takes not but from itself.*
> *Love possesses not nor would it be possessed;*
> *for love is sufficient unto love.*
> —KAHLIL GIBRAN, *The Prophet*

The Real Wedding

Lalla, you've wandered so many places
Trying to find your husband!
Now at last, inside the walls
Of this body-house, in the heart-shrine,
You discover where he lives.
—LALLA, *Naked Song*

The metaphor of the Beloved that runs through every page of *The Invisible Wedding* is to remind us to look to the One for love, not the ego and its incessant external quest. The love of the Beloved alone—closer to us than our own breath—is undying and unconditional. As the Master reiterated in every conceivable gesture, bond with the Beloved and enjoy! Be touched in every cell by the Beloved, and we will find ourselves touching a joy beyond anything in the world. Meet another who equally looks to the Beloved, and a rare spiritual jewel is born!

A question can arise in the mind: When we know that all love is within us—and is truly what we are—what's the point of being in relationship? The answer is extraordinarily simple: Relationship makes possible the Dance. Without the interconnected opposites of yin/yang, pleasure/pain, self/other, dual/nondual, Life cannot happen. Relationship is the instrument through which the Beloved, in all its disguises, dances. Lovers, in their hearts' passionate exploration, are constantly thrown out onto the razor's edge of the non-dual. In our deepest moments we know (without knowing we know) that there is only one heart here. But it cannot last. No sooner does unity dawn than, with a simple self-conscious thought, we are thrown back into the realm of duality. It is a cycle of expansion and contraction, Spirit and form that goes on forever. We are separate and one. This is the dance of Life, the great Mystery. It is this delicious Mystery that devours us at the depths of human love. Relationships, with all their sweat and blood, are a gift to be celebrated, not denied. Each one, however messy or awkward at times, points us toward the One Heart behind the many.

Love cannot be gotten from another. But something of its essence can be shared. It has been a joy for us to attempt to share this essence with our readers. May all beings be happy! May all beings be filled with peace!

Lovers don't finally meet somewhere.
They're in each other all along.
—Rumi